"This series is a tremendous resource for those wanting to study and teach the Bible with an understanding of how the gospel is woven throughout Scripture. Here are gospel-minded pastors and scholars doing gospel business from all the Scriptures. This is a biblical and theological feast preparing God's people to apply the entire Bible to all of life with heart and mind wholly committed to Christ's priorities."

BRYAN CHAPELL, pastor; author, *Christ-Centered Preaching* and *Christ-Centered Worship*

"Mark Twain may have smiled when he wrote to a friend, 'I didn't have time to write you a short letter, so I wrote you a long letter.' But the truth of Twain's remark remains serious and universal, because well-reasoned, compact writing requires extra time and extra hard work. And this is what we have in the Crossway Bible study series *Knowing the Bible*. The skilled authors and notable editors provide the contours of each book of the Bible as well as the grand theological themes that bind them together as one Book. Here, in a 12-week format, are carefully wrought studies that will ignite the mind and the heart."

R. KENT HUGHES, Senior Pastor Emeritus, College Church, Wheaton, Illinois

"*Knowing the Bible* brings together a gifted team of Bible teachers to produce a high-quality series of study guides. The coordinated focus of these materials is unique: biblical content, provocative questions, systematic theology, practical application, and the gospel story of God's grace presented all the way through Scripture."

PHILIP G. RYKEN, President, Wheaton College

"These *Knowing the Bible* volumes provide a significant and very welcome variation on the general run of inductive Bible studies. This series provides substantial instruction, as well as teaching through the very questions that are asked. *Knowing the Bible* then goes even further by showing how any given text links with the gospel, the whole Bible, and the formation of theology. I heartily endorse this orientation of individual books to the whole Bible and the gospel, and I applaud the demonstration that sound theology was not something invented later by Christians, but is right there in the pages of Scripture."

GRAEME L. GOLDSWORTHY, former lecturer in Old Testament, Biblical Theology, and Hermeneutics, Moore Theological College

"What a gift to earnest, Bible-loving, Bible-searching believers! The organization and structure of the Bible study format presented through the *Knowing the Bible* series is so well conceived. Students of the Word are led to understand the content of passages through perceptive, guided questions, and they are given rich insights and application all along the way in the brief but illuminating sections that conclude each study. What potential growth in depth and breadth of understanding these studies offer! One can only pray that vast numbers of believers will discover more of God and the beauty of his Word through these rich studies."

BRUCE A. WARE, T. Rupert and Lucille Coleman Professor of Christian Theology, The Southern Baptist Theological Seminary

KNOWING THE BIBLE

Douglas Sean O'Donnell, Series Editor

• • • • • •

Genesis
Exodus
Leviticus
Numbers
Deuteronomy
Joshua
Judges
Ruth and Esther
1–2 Samuel
1–2 Kings
1–2 Chronicles
Ezra and Nehemiah
Job
Psalms
Proverbs
Ecclesiastes
Song of Solomon
Isaiah
Jeremiah
Lamentations, Habakkuk, and Zephaniah
Ezekiel
Daniel
Hosea
Joel, Amos, and Obadiah
Jonah, Micah, and Nahum
Haggai, Zechariah, and Malachi
Matthew
Mark
Luke
John
Acts
Romans
1 Corinthians
2 Corinthians
Galatians
Ephesians
Philippians
Colossians and Philemon
1–2 Thessalonians
1–2 Timothy and Titus
Hebrews
James
1–2 Peter and Jude
1–3 John
Revelation

The Ten Commandments
The Miracles of Jesus
The Parables of Jesus
Jesus' Speech on the Mount of Olives
The Sermon on the Mount
Jesus' Farewell Discourse

• • • • • •

DOUGLAS SEAN O'DONNELL (PhD, University of Aberdeen) is the Senior Vice President of Bible Editorial at Crossway. He is the author and editor of more than a dozen books, including *The Beginning and End of Wisdom*; *The Pastor's Book*; *The Song of Solomon* and *Matthew* in the Preaching the Word commentary series; and *Psalms* and *The Parables of Jesus* in the Knowing the Bible series. He also contributed *Song of Solomon* and *Job* to the ESV Expository Commentary.

THE MIRACLES OF JESUS

A 12-WEEK STUDY

Edward W. Klink III and Casey F. Ehlers

WHEATON, ILLINOIS

Dedicated to our two sisters in the Lord, who "receive the word with all eagerness, examining the Scriptures daily to see if these things were so" (Acts 17:11)

Alberta Grossen and Pat Frederick

Knowing the Bible: The Miracles of Jesus, A 12-Week Study

Published by Crossway
1300 Crescent Street
Wheaton, Illinois 60187

Cover design: Simplicated Studio

First printing 2025

Printed in the United States of America

All emphases in Scripture quotations have been added by the author.

Trade paperback ISBN: 978-1-4335-9505-9

EPub ISBN: 978-1-4335-9507-3
PDF ISBN: 978-1-4335-9506-6

Crossway is a publishing ministry of Good News Publishers.

VP 35 34 33 32 31 30 29 28 27 26 25
15 14 13 12 11 10 9 8 7 6 5 4 3 2 1

Table of Contents

Series Preface: Douglas Sean O'Donnell 6

Week 1: Overview (John 20:30–31).. 9

Week 2: Jesus Turns Water into Wine (John 2:1–12)...................... 15

Week 3: Jesus Feeds the Five Thousand (Mark 6:30–44) 23

Week 4: Jesus Heals the Paralytic (Luke 5:17–26)......................... 31

Week 5: Jesus Heals the Demon-Possessed (Luke 8:26–39)............... 39

Week 6: Jesus Curses the Fig Tree (Mark 11:12–25)....................... 47

Week 7: Jesus Calms the Storm (Mark 4:35–41) 55

Week 8: Jesus Walks on Water (Matthew 14:22–33)....................... 63

Week 9: Jesus Reveals His Glory (Matthew 17:1–13)...................... 71

Week 10: Jesus Raises the Dead (John 11:1–57)........................... 79

Week 11: Jesus Rises from the Dead (John 20:1–18)........................ 87

Week 12: Summary and Conclusion.. 95

SERIES PREFACE

KNOWING THE BIBLE, as the title indicates, was created to help readers know and understand the meaning, the message, and the God of the Bible. This series was created and edited by Lane Dennis and Dane Ortlund, and J. I. Packer served as the theological editor. Dr. Packer has gone to be with the Lord, Lane has retired as CEO and president of Crossway, and Dane now serves as senior pastor of Naperville (Illinois) Presbyterian Church. We are so grateful for their labors in overseeing the first forty-plus volumes of this series! To honor and expand upon their idea, we are continuing the series, focusing on key sections from Scripture, such as the Ten Commandments and the Sermon on the Mount.

Each volume in the series consists of twelve units that progressively take the reader through a clear, concise, and deep study of certain portions of Scripture. The material works best for a small group, as the questions are designed for good interactive group discussion. Even so, an individual could easily use the material for a personal Bible study as well.

Week 1 provides an overview of the section or sections of Scripture to be studied, which includes placing the text into its larger context (e.g., the Sermon on the Mount within the Gospel of Matthew), providing key historical background, and offering some questions to get started. Weeks 2–12 each have the following features: a summary of how the text fits into the rest of Scripture ("The Place of the Passage"), a summary sentence on the main theme ("The Big Picture"), and ten or so questions ("Reflection and Discussion Questions"). Moreover, each unit highlights the role of the gospel of grace in each text ("Gospel Glimpses"), identifies whole-Bible themes ("Whole-Bible Connections"), pinpoints Christian doctrines ("Theological Soundings"), defines key terms ("Definitions"), and allows space to respond ("Personal Implications").

Lastly, to help readers understand the Bible better, we urge readers to use the ESV Bible and the *ESV Study Bible*, which are available in various print and digital formats, including online editions at esv.org. The *Knowing the Bible* series is also available online.

May our gracious God, who has generously given his Spirit and his Word, use this study to grow his people in their knowledge and love of the Father, Son, and Spirit.

Douglas Sean O'Donnell
Series Editor

WEEK 1: OVERVIEW

John 20:30–31

Getting Acquainted

Many people who live in the Western world today think of a miracle as something that occurs contrary to nature. A more accurate definition, however, is the way Augustine explained it: a miracle is an occurrence that is contrary to that which is *known* of nature. Augustine's reasoning is driven by the biblical fact that the world is not a closed system. Even the word *nature* speaks in a less-than-biblical manner. Scripture makes clear that the world is God's creation. That which we might refer to naively as nature from our perspective is, from God's perspective (and that of the Bible), the operations of the world that God powerfully created and purposefully sustains. Miracles, then, might be defined as the "extraordinary operations" of God that intervene in the seemingly natural operations of creation. In that sense they are unmistakably more powerful and purposeful regarding that which they point to and communicate. This might explain why the arrival of Jesus ("when the fullness of time had come," Gal. 4:4) was surrounded by so many miracles—or, as the Gospel of John describes them, signs[1] that "manifested [Jesus'] glory" (John 2:11).

The four Gospels provide the official account of the miracles of Jesus that he accomplished during his time on earth almost two thousand years ago. Jesus healed sick people, calmed violent storms, exorcised demons, fed multitudes, and walked on water. These miracles served an important purpose in his earthly ministry, and still today (as recorded in Matthew, Mark, Luke, and John) serve an important purpose in Christian formation and discipleship. It is far too common, however, for Christians to think of miracles as problems to be resolved in our modern world. It is as though miracles are merely to serve a utilitarian purpose for Christian apologetics. While the study of the historical fact and reasonableness of miracles has its place, the biblical accounts focus less on the "how" and more on the "why"—not the proof but the purpose of Jesus' miracles. The primary intention of the miracles of Jesus is to teach every disciple—those who witnessed the miracle in person and those today who read the testimony of the apostles—about the person and work of Jesus. A study on miracles, then, should be driven by a concern not merely to defend Jesus' mighty acts but to understand them, even to be formed by them.

It is helpful when interpreting a miracle account to break it into three related parts: (1) *the setting*, which introduces the characters, context, and crisis in need of resolution; (2) *the miracle*, in which Jesus performs an "extraordinary operation" of *sign*ificance; and (3) *the conclusion*, in which the narrative provides an interpretation of the work or the Worker (Jesus) in implicit and explicit ways. The questions included in each chapter will follow this structure.

Placing It in the Larger Story

Throughout the Old Testament God performed miracles or empowered others to do so on his behalf. The primary example is the exodus[2] (Ex. 1–18), which served as a foundational miracle in the unfolding biblical story and communication of God's redeeming work. The exodus offers something like a trailer for the rest of the biblical story and serves as a formal introduction to the work Jesus would ultimately accomplish. That which occurred in the exodus is echoed in the Gospels, as Jesus—the "new Moses"—offers full and final redemption for God's people from their enslavement to sin and death. In Exodus God calls the miracles "signs" (Ex. 4:9; 7:3). John uses the same language in his Gospel to speak of Jesus' miracles, and with these "signs" he communicates truths about Jesus and summons people to place faith in him.

Over forty miracles of Jesus are recorded in the Gospels, with each communicating particular truths about Jesus and offering different challenges to the reader. The message communicated by each can be more easily grasped if we understand the nature of the miracle. While many have classified miracles simply by their historical type (e.g., nature miracle), C. S. Lewis offers a helpful additional classification to explain their significance: the miracle's place in biblical history in relation to the old creation and the new creation.[3] Miracles that "sign" with operations fitting the current world are miracles of the old creation, whereas those that "sign" with operations fitting the coming world are miracles of the new creation. The following chart lists the miracles in relation to both types.

Types of Miracles	Miracles of the Old Creation	Miracles of the New Creation
Miracles of Fertility	Water to wine (God's provision for his creation)	
Miracles of Healing	Curing the sick (God's healing of his creation)	
Miracles of Destruction	Withering a fig tree (God's judgment of his creation)	
Miracles of Dominion	Stilling a storm (God's control over his creation)	Walking on water (future reality of a new human nature)
Miracles of Reversal		Raising of Lazarus (God's renewal of his creation)
Miracles of Glorification		Jesus' resurrection (new creation's inauguration)

This two-part classification reveals the ministerial authority of Jesus and his active work in the present world, as well as the purpose behind his ministry that focuses on the world to come. The miracles of Jesus, using the unfolding biblical narrative as their framework, depict the gospel's progression from Genesis to Revelation, representing the ultimate and true exodus. These miracles offer profound insights into Jesus' mission and message, which are centered on the gospel, the "good news" that God has been revealing to the world since the beginning. For Christians today the miracles of Jesus provide specific lessons about God's nature, his actions in the world, his care for the church, and the ultimate restoration of all things in the new creation.

Key Verse

"Now Jesus did many other signs in the presence of the disciples, which are not written in this book; but these are written so that you may believe that Jesus is the Christ, the Son of God, and that by believing you may have life in his name" (John 20:30–31).

Date and Historical Background

The four Gospels offer apostolic, eyewitness testimony to the life and ministry of Jesus (on the dates of Jesus' ministry and crucifixion see *ESV Study Bible*, pages

1809–1810). While contemporary readers may raise philosophical questions about the possibility of miracles from their modern perspective, neither those in the ancient world nor confessing Christians who accept the authority of Scripture truly doubt the veracity of the miraculous accounts. Not only do the miracles of Jesus fit comfortably in the worldview of the first-century world in which Jesus lived, but they also sit comfortably in the domain of Jesus' authority as the incarnate Son of God (see Col. 1:15–20). The miracles of Jesus are clearly expressing Jesus as the fulfillment of Old Testament prophecies regarding the promised Messiah, who would enact God's intentions for his people and his creation. As they are recorded in the four Gospels, therefore, the miracles of Jesus offer a primary interpretation of the person of Jesus and his ministry in the world.

Outline

- I. Miracles of the Old Creation
  - A. Jesus Turns Water into Wine (John 2:1–12)
  - B. Jesus Feeds the Five Thousand (Mark 6:30–44)
  - C. Jesus Heals the Paralytic (Luke 5:17–26)
  - D. Jesus Heals the Demon-Possessed (Luke 8:26–39)
  - E. Jesus Curses the Fig Tree (Mark 11:12–25)
  - F. Jesus Calms the Storm (Mark 4:35–41)
- II. Miracles of the New Creation
  - A. Jesus Walks on Water (Matthew 14:22–33)
  - B. Jesus Reveals His Glory (Matthew 17:1–13)
  - C. Jesus Raises the Dead (John 11:1–57)
  - D. Jesus Rises from the Dead (John 20:1–18)

As You Get Started

Do you believe that Jesus performed miracles? Are there any of his miracles that you struggle to believe?

Of all Jesus' miracles, is there one that stands out to you? Why do you think that particular miracle stands out to you?

Are there any of Jesus' miracles that are confusing to you? How could fitting Jesus' miracles into the broader story of Scripture (e.g., the exodus, new creation) help explain their purpose?

Jesus' miracles are not just for those who witnessed them in the flesh; they are for every Christian at all times. Can you think of some ways in which Jesus' miracles could inform Christians today about how we ought to live in and love the world around us?

As You Finish This Unit . . .

As you prepare to focus on the miracles of Jesus, it might be helpful for you to read at least one of the Gospels in its entirety. Consider the ways that the narratives about Jesus direct the reader to see the significance of his person and work. This will give you the necessary context to begin a study of the miracles of Jesus, which are couched in the larger narratives of the four Gospels. And spend some time praying that the Lord would open your eyes to see the wondrous truths presented to his people through the miracles of Jesus.

Definitions

[1] **Signs** – Miracles that attest to Jesus' identity as Messiah and Son of God and lead unbelievers to faith.

[2] **Exodus, the** – The departure of the people of Israel from Egypt and their journey to Mount Sinai under Moses' leadership (Exodus 1–19; Numbers 33). The exodus demonstrated God's power and providence for his people, who had been enslaved by the Egyptians. The annual festival of Passover commemorates God's final plague upon the Egyptians, resulting in their release from Egypt.

[3] **New creation** – The world to come (Heb. 2:5), which stands in contrast with the sin-laden world in this "present evil age" (see Gal. 1:4; 6:15).

Week 2: Jesus Turns Water into Wine

John 2:1–12

The Place of the Passage

While the Gospels do not reveal a precise chronological order of the miracles of Jesus, the Gospel of John specifically calls Jesus' miracle at the wedding in Cana the "first of his signs" (John 2:11). In the ministry of Jesus this miracle seems to take place right after the calling of the disciples, at a family wedding to which he and his disciples have been invited. In John's Gospel this passage follows a theologically rich introduction to Jesus that employs a prologue and two passages to set the ministerial context for his person and work (1:1–51). The miracle opens the second chapter of John and serves as the formal beginning of the ministry of Jesus. In addition to its purpose in the narrative this remarkable story is loaded with very intentional biblical symbolism. This includes a few short statements from Jesus that can be difficult to understand but serve readers by helping them connect the miracle beyond this particular wedding to the larger marriage taking place between God and man. This is not only a miracle of fertility (i.e., "provision") but also an "old creation" miracle, which means it is a sign with operations fitting the current world. In this miracle Jesus reveals a central purpose of his ministry and how he intends to unite the world to God through his purifying work.

The Big Picture

Jesus has been sent by his Father to purify the children of God, preparing the church, the bride of Christ, to receive its bridegroom.

Reflection and Discussion

Read through the complete passage for this study, John 2:1–12. Then review the following questions and record your responses. (For further background, see the *ESV Study Bible*, pages 2022–2023, or visit esv.org.)

The Setting (John 2:1–5)

Weddings in the ancient world did not occur over a single afternoon but lasted seven days, and it was common for a teacher's disciples to be invited (2:1–2). How might Jesus, the incarnate Word (1:14) and teacher of new disciples, have been torn between his divine identity and mission and his role as a son and family member?

The seemingly odd response of Jesus in 2:4 is an ancient way of seeking to distance oneself politely from the needs of another, in this case the need for wine (2:3). For Jesus the need of his mother is a lesser priority than the mission of his Father, which he describes as "my hour."[1] According to John what were the purposes for which God the Father had sent Jesus the Son into the world?

How does the setting of the miracle lay both needs at the feet of Jesus: the mother's request to her son for wine at a family wedding and the Father's mission for the Son for a much larger family (the church)?

The Miracle (John 2:6–8)

What was the religious purpose of the water for Jewish rites of purification[2] (read Mark 7:3–4), and why is it significant that Jesus changes that particular water into wine (for help see "Final Purification" in *Gospel Glimpses* below)?

If the water for purification reflects God's provision for his people in the old covenant (in the Old Testament), how does its transformation into wine reflect God's fuller provision for his people in the new covenant?

How does Jesus address both his mother's desire and his Father's mission when he turns the water intended for the Jewish rites of purification into celebratory wine for the wedding?

The Conclusion (John 2:9–12)

The anonymous master of the feast and the bridegroom are clueless about the appearance of the wine. How does Jesus fulfill the roles of both characters, especially in regard to the bridegroom? Moreover, how does this fit the depiction of Jesus elsewhere in Scripture (e.g., Eph. 5:22–33; Rev. 19:6–9)?

The apparent strategy mentioned in John 2:10 is that the better wine would get used first until the palate had been numbed and cheaper wine could be used unnoticeably. How does this reversal reflect the way in which Jesus gives the world the final and fullest provision of God in redemptive history?

In light of the purpose of miracles, what does this miracle teach us about the person of Jesus (who he is) or the work of Jesus (what he has done for us)?

Read through the following three sections on *Gospel Glimpses*, *Whole-Bible Connections*, and *Theological Soundings*. Then take time to consider the *Personal Implications* these sections have for you.

Gospel Glimpses

FINAL PURIFICATION. The implications for stone jars in Jewish purity laws (e.g., clay jars could become unclean) and the water for ceremonial washing traditions become obsolete the moment Jesus appears on the scene. He alone is the perfect and pure sacrifice, fulfilling every purity law. And Jesus alone offers the perfect and final ceremony washing, a washing "with the Holy Spirit" (John 1:33; 13:8). When Jesus transforms the ceremonial water into celebratory wine, he communicates this truth to the wedding guests and, through John, to all Christians.

CHRIST'S HOUR. The term *hour* in John is a technical term that points to the death of Jesus on the cross (John 4:21; 7:30) but also more generally includes his resurrection (5:25, 28) and ascension (13:1). Jesus' seemingly odd interaction with his mother regarding wine for the wedding is due to the fact that Jesus has a clear and more significant mission from his Father required for a greater sacred wedding—the marriage between Jesus the bridegroom and his bride, the church (Eph. 5:22–33). Not only the ministry of Jesus but also the clear message of Scripture present to Christians the importance of his death, resurrection, and ascension. Christians are tempted, like Jesus' mother was, to desire Jesus' working on their behalf in a variety of material ways. But, while Jesus does provide for our physical needs, we should never forget the primary purpose Jesus has been assigned to accomplish on our behalf. His divinely appointed hour saves us—body and soul—from sin, death, and eternal judgment.

Whole-Bible Connections

THE GREATEST WEDDING. Through Jesus' fulfilling the role of the master of the feast and especially the bridegroom, this miracle story teaches the reader to see the far grander wedding depicted through Scripture: the wedding between God and humanity. The church, the bride of Christ, has enjoined herself to the true bridegroom, Jesus Christ, and waits for the full and final celebration to begin—the future marriage supper of the Lamb (Rev. 19:6–9).

THE GOOD WINE. In the Old Testament an abundance of wine is used regularly as a symbol for the coming kingdom of God (e.g., Amos 9:13–14; cf. Gen. 49:11). In the context of this miracle recorded in John the abundance of wine (six massive containers filled to the top!) declares that Jesus' person and work are the full blessing of God's activity in the world. As the prophet Isaiah foretold, "The Lord of hosts will make for all peoples a feast of rich food, a feast of well-aged wine . . . wine well refined. . . . It will be said on that day, 'Behold, this is our God; we have waited for him, that he might save us. This is the LORD; we have waited for him; let us be glad and rejoice in his salvation'" (Isa. 25:6, 9).

Theological Soundings

THE MISSION OF THE FATHER. The clear bond between Jesus and his mother is defined properly in this passage by the eternal bond between Jesus and his Father. Jesus carefully and respectfully locates his response to his mother within the loving confines of the mission he has received from his Father. The distance Jesus must place between his mother and himself is an obedient expression of the love of God. The call of every Christian is to make the will and wisdom of God the foundation of every human plan and purpose; it is to have the petition "your will be done" (Matt. 6:10) be the scaffolding of every thought and of every decision and action.

GLORY MANIFESTED. This miracle story states explicitly that the "signs" of Jesus "manifested his glory" (John 2:11). In Scripture the glory of God is his majestic splendor and power, as well as the manifestation of his being, nature, and presence. Through miracles this reality about God's glory is made "manifest" in a manner accessible to human experience. While the fullest experience of God's glory will have to wait for the new creation, the miracles of Jesus allow Christians to experience an aspect of the worthiness and weightiness of God, the God-ness of God. Christians are correct in pursuing the glory of God, giving God the worth of his God-ness in our words and deeds, and in Christ and through the Spirit they can even see God's glory in real, even if partial, ways.

Personal Implications

Take some time to reflect on what you have learned from your study of John 2:1–12 and how it might apply to your own life today. Make notes below on the personal implications for your walk with the Lord of the (1) *Gospel Glimpses*, (2) *Whole-Bible Connections*, (3) *Theological Soundings*, and (4) this passage as a whole.

1. Gospel Glimpses

2. Whole-Bible Connections

3. Theological Soundings

4. John 2:1–12

As You Finish This Unit . . .

Jesus, our bridegroom, ministers to his bride, the church. Bring out the celebratory wine! Take a moment to look back through this study and reflect on the key things the Lord may be teaching you.

Definitions

[1] **Hour, the** – A technical term in the Gospel of John for the climactic ministerial acts of Jesus: his death, resurrection, and ascension.

[2] **Purification** – The religious act of removing spiritual uncleanliness, as defined by the purity laws of the Old Testament, by means of prescribed ceremonies or rites.

Week 3: Jesus Feeds the Five Thousand

Mark 6:30–44

The Place of the Passage

Mark's Gospel situates Jesus' feeding of the five thousand within a series of well-known events in the life of Christ. The immediate details of chapter 6 place the miracle during a season of ministry in which Jesus is traveling between villages to teach (see Mark 6:6). Due to Jesus' rejection at his hometown of Nazareth the narrative shift marks a new season of ministry outside Galilee (see *ESV Study Bible* notes Mark 6:7–8:26 on page 1904). Chronologically this would place the miracle toward the end of Jesus' public ministry. It should also be noted that this is the only pre-resurrection miracle that appears in all four Gospels (cf. Matt. 14:13–21; Luke 9:12–17; John 6:1–15). Also connected to this miracle is the sending out of the twelve and their return (Mark 6:7–13, 30) and the death of John the Baptist (Mark 6:14–29). This miracle, along with the previous week's miracle (see Week 2: Jesus Turns Water into Wine), is a miracle of fertility (i.e., "provision") and therefore an old creation miracle, which means it is a sign with operations fitting the current world. In this miracle Jesus displays his compassion for people as he offers hospitality and provision to his disciples and the crowds.

The Big Picture

Jesus, the Shepherd, demonstrates compassion toward the sheep by providing the hospitality of his common grace for his people.

Reflection and Discussion

Read through the complete passage for this study, Mark 6:30–44. Then review the following questions and record your responses. (For further background, see the *ESV Study Bible*, pages 1905–1906, or visit esv.org.)

The Setting (Mark 6:30–37)

By referring to Jesus' disciples as "the apostles"[1] (6:30) and recounting how the people "recognized them" (6:33) Mark shows how the disciples share in the popularity of Jesus. What do you think leads to Jesus' concern for the hunger of the people (6:34), whereas his disciples argue that it was not their problem (6:37)?

The narrator says specifically that Jesus "had compassion on [the crowds of people], because they were like sheep without a shepherd" (6:34)? What does this reveal about Jesus' character and mission? And how does the fact that Jesus both teaches (6:34) and feeds them (6:37) reflect compassion?

The disciples counter Jesus' command to feed the crowds with an argument about money (see 6:37; "two hundred denarii" are about half a year's wages).

How reasonable is the disciples' argument? How might Christians today be tempted to let money and finances affect ministry decisions?

The Miracle (Mark 6:38–41)

As the Creator (John 1:3), Jesus could have created food out of nothing, but he chooses to use the minimal resources available to him, even from a person in the crowd (Mark 6:38). Why might Jesus have chosen this way to provide, and how does God still provide for his people today through the resources that already exist?

Why do you think Jesus commanded the people to be divided into groups (6:39–40)? If we imagine those groupings as churches (the average church in America is between fifty and one hundred people), how does this scene reflect the way Jesus provides for every local church?

Jesus took the five loaves and two fish and blessed them (6:41). How does this provide an example for Christians to follow in the practice of thanksgiving? What are you thankful for today?

The Conclusion (Mark 6:42–44)

Mark wants the reader to know that after the miraculous feeding every person in the crowd is "satisfied" (6:42). How is that significant, and how does Jesus, the Shepherd, still satisfy his sheep today?

The small resources result in an abundance of leftovers (6:43)—one basket for each doubting disciple to carry! What might the excess loaves and fish teach us about Jesus and his provision?

In light of the purpose of miracles, what does this miracle teach Christians about the person of Jesus (who he is) or the work of Jesus (what he has done for us)?

Read through the following three sections on *Gospel Glimpses*, *Whole-Bible Connections*, and *Theological Soundings*. Then take time to consider the *Personal Implications* these sections have for you.

Gospel Glimpses

JESUS LOVES. Jesus demonstrates his compassion in two separate ways during this miracle of fertility. First, he notices the confusion and helplessness of the crowds and responds by drawing near and caring for them (6:34). This caring includes teaching the people about the things of God, as well as caring for their physical needs. Jesus truly cares for his people in word and in deed. Second, Jesus cares for the spiritual formation of his followers, whom he invites to share in the shepherding of the crowd. In this way Jesus teaches the church that they are not a cul-de-sac of God's grace but a conduit. As with the loaves and the fish, God uses the minimal resources of his people to provide his love to the world. Yet it is always his love given us through Jesus by the Holy Spirit, for "we love because he first loved us" (1 John 4:19).

JESUS FEEDS THE HUNGRY. This miracle makes a connection between ministering to the soul and ministering to the body. Ministry for Jesus always involves the whole person. Yet Christians are tempted to pick between the soul and the body, between soul-saving and physical work. But what "God has joined together, let not man separate" (Matt. 19:6). Even more, the gospel itself is about Jesus' feeding the hungry: "Blessed are those who hunger and thirst for righteousness, for they shall be satisfied" (Matt. 5:6); "They shall hunger no more. . . . The Lamb in the midst of the throne will be their shepherd" (Rev. 7:16–17). Jesus will always feed his people, with loaves of wheat and as the bread of life (John 6:35).

Whole-Bible Connections

SHEEP WITHOUT A SHEPHERD. Jesus had compassion on the crowds because they were "like sheep without a shepherd" (Mark 6:34). This is an allusion to several passages in the Old Testament that mention directly the failure of Israel's leaders (cf. Num. 27:17; Ezek. 34:4–5). Jesus is a leader like none before and will provide fully for the needs of his people. This truth has long and progressive unveiling in the biblical story, with one of its clearest expressions when God promises an offspring leader to the shepherd-king David in 2 Samuel 7:11–16. The Old Testament kingship of Israel points to the coming King, Jesus, a faithful leader of his people who is full of compassion and grace.

THE SHEPHERD. In Psalm 23:1–4 we see a beautiful picture of God's care of his people through the image of a shepherd's tending to his flock. Sheep are easily scared animals, and the work of a shepherd includes constant attention, patience, and guidance. One aspect of this vocation is the reassurance of safety, which even includes encouraging the sheep to lie down in the pasture (see Ps. 23:2). Jesus enacts the image of the Good Shepherd by guiding the wayward crowds toward trusting him as Shepherd in having them sit down in the grass (Mark 6:39). The comparison is stark and serves as a message to Christ's church. Jesus will always care for his sheep in this way, for "The LORD is my shepherd; I shall not want. He makes me lie down in green pastures" (Ps. 23:1).

Theological Soundings

COMMON GRACE. This crowd inevitably consists of many different people with a multitude of postures toward Jesus. Regardless of these people's motives, Jesus has compassion on them and gives this hungry crowd his food. Jesus uses this miracle to demonstrate his benevolent compassion on all his image bearers—he does not pick favorites or exclude skeptics. His posture toward the crowds is one that should be emulated by his followers as we live, work, and minister in the world. This benevolence reflects God's common grace, or the gifts of God as Creator. Just as the Father "makes his sun rise on the evil and on the good, and sends rain on the just and on the unjust" (Matt. 5:45), so he gives loaves from the crops and fish from the sea to all people.

SPECIAL GRACE. Just as Jesus gives bread to the hungry, he is also the bread of life (John 6:35), which means he also provides a special grace that comes only by faith in him. If common grace is a reflection of God as Creator (think *C* for Creator), then special grace is a reflection of God as Savior (think *S* for Savior). Special grace is accomplished only through the death, resurrection, and ascension of Jesus. Special grace is a grace for his disciples, the grace that forms and shapes them—a covenantal love for his followers by which they have unlimited access to Jesus as their Lord. The ministry of the church is strengthened when we recognize all things as coming from and reflecting either God's common or special grace, for God is both Creator and Savior.

Personal Implications

Take some time to reflect on what you have learned from your study of Mark 6:30–44 and how it might apply to your own life today. Make notes below on the personal implications for your walk with the Lord of the (1) *Gospel Glimpses*, (2) *Whole-Bible Connections*, (3) *Theological Soundings*, and (4) this passage as a whole.

1. Gospel Glimpses

2. Whole-Bible Connections

3. Theological Soundings

4. Mark 6:30–44

As You Finish This Unit . . .

Jesus, the Shepherd, demonstrates his tender compassion and provision. Reflect on this truth in your own personal life and respond in prayers of adoration and thanksgiving.

Definitions

[1] **Apostle** – "One who is sent," and who is an official representative of another. In the New Testament the word refers specifically to those whom Jesus chose to represent him.

Week 4: Jesus Heals the Paralytic

Luke 5:17–26

The Place of the Passage

The Gospels may appear to record events from the life of Jesus in a random manner, with little to no connection between them, but this is hardly the case. A general rule is that the narratives in the same context are linked thematically, that is, by topic. This is clearly the case in Luke 5, wherein two men—a leper and a paralytic—are healed by Jesus. Both of these serve to depict the biblical relations between physical and spiritual sickness. This is notable, for the theme of sin is formally introduced in the story preceding these two miracles, as Peter is called forth by Jesus and attempts to decline Jesus' invitation by calling himself a "sinful man" (Luke 5:8). Peter's self-diagnosis is impressed upon him by the miraculous catch of fish that Jesus gifts to him and his companions (Luke 5:4–6). The two healing accounts that follow offer a biblical answer to Peter's crisis, explaining that Jesus is the healer of humanity in every way. Jesus makes this claim explicit in the healing of the paralytic not only when he shows the connection between the body and the soul but also when he declares himself the ultimate authority over both. This is not only a miracle of healing but also an "old creation" miracle, which means it is a sign with operations fitting the current world. In this miracle Jesus reveals an important purpose of his ministry and the way in which he intends to redeem his creation from the sicknesses of sin.

The Big Picture

Jesus is the healer of humanity, the one who has the authority to heal the body and to forgive sins, both of which address our fallen creation.

Reflection and Discussion

Read through the complete passage for this study, Luke 5:17–26. Then review the following questions and record your responses. (For further background, see the *ESV Study Bible*, page 1960, or visit esv.org.)

The Setting (Luke 5:17–21)

Why does verse 17 inform the reader that "the power of the Lord was with [Jesus] to heal?" What does this teach us about the authority shared between or given to God the Son by God the Father?

What does the aggressive manner in which the men bring the paralyzed man into the house communicate to us? How does verse 20 provide Jesus' interpretation of their actions?

Why does Jesus see the paralyzed man and first address his sin (5:20)? What does this teach us about the nature of sin?

The Pharisees (the spiritual influencers of Israel) and the teachers of the law (or, scribes; the biblical scholars of Israel), introduced in verse 17, later challenge Jesus' ministry toward the paralytic (5:21). Why do they have a problem with what Jesus says?

The Miracle (Luke 5:22–24)

Before Jesus performs the miracle of physical restoration, he poses a question that explains the purpose of the miracle. How would you answer Jesus' question in verse 23?

Why does Jesus want to make clear that he can heal the body and the soul (5:24), and why is his authority over both aspects important?

The Conclusion (Luke 5:25–26)

Jesus commands the paralytic to rise, and verse 25 says that the paralytic does so "immediately." How does this detail give insight into Jesus' power and authority?

The response of the man and all those present is overwhelmingly positive: "They glorified God" (5:26). What does it mean that they "glorified God," and what does this collective response communicate to us?

In light of the purpose of miracles, what does this miracle teach Christians about the person of Jesus (who he is) or the work of Jesus (what he has done for us)?

Read through the following three sections on *Gospel Glimpses*, *Whole-Bible Connections*, and *Theological Soundings*. Then take time to consider the *Personal Implications* these sections have for you.

Gospel Glimpses

BODY AND SOUL. The tendency to view the ministry of Jesus as pursuing the healing of our souls only is challenged by this miracle. This should be quite obvious, since Jesus' work of redemption requires his body: "He himself bore our sins in his body on the tree. . . . By his wounds you have been healed" (1 Pet. 2:24). This rebukes in us any "spiritual" talk that diminishes the ways in which the work of Jesus involves our bodies. The message of salvation that Scripture announces involves not only the soul (1 Pet. 1:9) but also the body, looking forward to a time when "death shall be no more, neither shall there be mourning, nor crying, nor pain anymore [nor any paralytics], for the former things have passed away" (Rev. 21:4). Praise be to God that Jesus works miracles of redemption in body and soul.

YOUR SINS ARE FORGIVEN. The first thing Jesus says when the paralytic man is placed before him is "Your sins are forgiven you" (Luke 5:20). To the ears of the Pharisees and scribes Jesus' statement is blasphemy, for it is a claim that only God can make (5:21). Their theology of sin is correct, but their knowledge of God is deficient, most notably as God the Son stands before them. This might explain why Jesus declares himself to be the authoritative Son of Man in verse 24. But the significant connection Jesus makes between healing and forgiveness[1] of sins must not be missed, and the connection is rooted in the gospel. Just as the "wages of sin is death" (Rom. 6:23), so the gift of God is the miracle of life, true healing. Sin is the source of the man's paralyzed body, and only the redeeming work of God can heal him.

Whole-Bible Connections

THE SON OF MAN HAS AUTHORITY. Jesus' favorite self-designation is "Son of Man." The title is used in Daniel 7:13–14, which describes one who, clothed by God with heavenly glory, is to exercise God's rule on earth. In the context of this miracle the title makes clear to the Pharisees and scribes—and to the readers—that there should be no questions regarding Jesus' authority either to forgive sins or to heal bodies. In fact, as Scripture gradually reveals, this was the assignment given to Jesus from the beginning.

THEY GLORIFIED GOD. In the full story of Scripture the glory[2] of God is the manifestation of his being, nature, and presence that is revealed and experienced by humanity (see Ex. 33:18–23). The end of this miracle account makes clear to the reader that all the participants have experienced God's glory. As stated previously, the conclusion of the story is where the message of a miracle is interpreted. The narrative explains that the former paralytic is "glorifying God" (Luke 5:25) on his walk home, and all the witnesses have amazement "seize them all" as they also "glorified God" and are even "filled with awe" (5:26). This is a very detailed account of the human experience of God's glory, and it is a foretaste of the pleasure and power to be known by all God's people in his intimate presence in the new creation (cf. Rev. 21:23).

Theological Soundings

THE POWER OF THE LORD. The above discussion of Jesus' authority as the "Son of Man" helps us make sense of the brief statement at the beginning of the miracle: "The power of the Lord was with him to heal" (Luke 5:17). What the religious leaders do not accept, but the paralyzed man and his friends believe (note 5:20), is that Jesus has been given this authority from God. Jesus, the second person of the Trinity, has been given this authority: "The Father . . . has given judgment to the Son" and "given him authority" (John 5:22, 27). As Jesus himself states, "All authority in heaven and on earth has been given to me" (Matt. 28:18). In this way Scripture teaches us that Jesus has all authority, so that both our bodies and our lives must be submitted to him.

FAITH. The narrative reveals to the reader that Jesus is impressed with the faith[3] of the friends of the paralytic. In contrast to the religious authorities, they believe in Jesus' ability and authority to heal. Scripture teaches us this directly ("Without faith it is impossible to please him, for whoever would draw near to God must believe that he exists and that he rewards those who seek him," Heb. 11:6). This biblical truth is like oxygen for our spiritual lives. The faithful disciple of Jesus places his faith in Jesus and trusts Jesus with his life.

Personal Implications

Take some time to reflect on what you have learned from your study of Luke 5:17–26 and how it might apply to your own life today. Make notes below on the personal implications for your walk with the Lord of the (1) *Gospel Glimpses*, (2) *Whole-Bible Connections*, (3) *Theological Soundings*, and (4) this passage as a whole.

1. Gospel Glimpses

2. Whole-Bible Connections

3. Theological Soundings

4. Luke 5:17–26

As You Finish This Unit . . .

May your faith be strengthened as you stand in awe of the fact that Jesus heals both the body and the soul, including the forgiveness of our sins. Take a moment to look back through this study and reflect on what you learned about Jesus the Healer and the ways in which he ministers to you.

Definitions

[1] **Forgiveness** – Release from guilt and the reestablishment of relationship. Forgiveness can be granted by God to human beings (Luke 24:47; 1 John 1:9) and by human beings to those who have wronged them (Matt. 18:21–22; Col. 3:13).

[2] **Glory** – The beauty of God gone public. The Scriptures are saturated with the theme of God's glory—a glory that shines brightest in the person and work of Jesus. The Bible testifies to the glory of God in eternity past (John 17:1, 4–5), in creation (Ps. 19:1; Isa. 43:6–7, 21; Col. 1:16–18), in redemption (Ps. 79:9; Jer. 14:7, 21; Rom. 3:23–26; 2 Cor. 4:4), and in eternity future (2 Thess. 1:10; Rev. 5:9; 21:23).

[3] **Faith** – Trust in or reliance upon something or someone despite a lack of concrete proof. Salvation, which is purely a work of God's grace, can be received only through faith (Rom. 5:2, Eph. 2:8–9). The writer of Hebrews calls on believers to emulate those who lived godly lives by faith (Hebrews 11).

Week 5: Jesus Heals the Demon-Possessed

Luke 8:26–39

The Place of the Passage

Our modern world has relegated the "spiritual forces of evil in the heavenly places" (Eph. 6:12) to movies and make-believe. This makes it more difficult for Christians to grasp the significance of biblical texts that speak about demons.[1] The Bible reveals the truth about our world, about a Creator and his creatures—including those in the spiritual realm. Human nature is drawn to inquire of such spiritual beings, but Scripture does not allow us to dwell on the details. It does, however, make clear that "spiritual forces of evil" challenge God and his people, the church. Just as human creatures can be agents of sin and death, so can spiritual creatures. Every place and person in creation has been stricken with sin's disease—even creatures in the heavenly places. This context is essential to grasping the encounter that takes place in Luke 8, wherein Jesus heals a man who "had demons" (Luke 8:27). In this powerful encounter the reader of Scripture is reminded that the sickness of sin extends deep into the spiritual realms of creation and that Jesus Christ alone has the authority to heal creation's spiritual sickness. This is not only a miracle of healing but also an "old creation" miracle, which means it is a sign with operations fitting the current world. In this miracle Jesus reveals a crucial purpose of his ministry and how he intends to redeem his creation from the spiritual forces of evil.

The Big Picture

Jesus has authority and power over every spiritual force of evil and darkness, and he delivers his people from the enslaving bonds of demonic powers and unclean spirits.

Reflection and Discussion

Read through the complete passage for this study, Luke 8:26–39. Then review the following questions and record your responses. (For further background, see the *ESV Study Bible*, page 1969, or visit esv.org.)

The Setting (Luke 8:26–29)

What is the biblical text describing when it says that the man "had demons" (8:27) and an "unclean spirit" (8:29) that "had seized him" (8:29)?

Do you believe in demons? Why or why not? Have you ever known someone who experienced some kind of demonic activity? What was it like?

Why do the demons respond to Jesus in the way that they do, and what does that communicate to us about Jesus (8:28)?

The Miracle (Luke 8:30–33)

Why does Jesus speak to the demons, and what does the demons' reaction to Jesus teach us about his authority over them?

What are the demons begging Jesus to do, and why do you think he grants their request (8:32)?

What does Jesus' authority over the demons mean for Christians today? How can we live with confidence that all demons are under the authority of our Lord Jesus Christ?

The Conclusion (Luke 8:34–39)

The narrative twice mentions the intense "fear" (8:35, 37) that the miracle induces in the herdsmen and townspeople. What does this reaction by the witnesses teach us about the significance of Jesus' actions?

Why does Jesus not allow the man he healed from demon possession to stay with him, and what is the significance of what Jesus tells him to do when he goes home (8:39)?

In light of the purpose of miracles what does this miracle teach Christians about the person of Jesus (who he is) or the work of Jesus (what he has done for us)?

Read through the following three sections on *Gospel Glimpses*, *Whole-Bible Connections*, and *Theological Soundings*. Then take time to consider the *Personal Implications* these sections have for you.

Gospel Glimpses

EVERY TONGUE CONFESS. The most honorific and theologically precise titles ascribed to Jesus in the Gospels are spoken not by the religious leaders of Israel or even his disciples but by demons! The demons know that Jesus, who is often addressed as "teacher" or "rabbi"—even by his disciples—should be properly addressed as "Son of the Most High God" (Luke 8:28). The demons address him with absolute reverence and submission, and their actions project what all creatures will someday do. After Jesus' suffering service for us God has exalted him over us so that every knee should bow and "every tongue confess that Jesus Christ is Lord" (Phil. 2:11). The message of the gospel includes both what Jesus has done but also who Jesus is. Jesus is indeed the Son of the Most High God!

INTO THE ABYSS. A remarkable insight is given to the reader when we hear the demons beg Jesus "not to command them to depart into the abyss" (Luke 8:31). In the larger context of Scripture the abyss is clearly the place of God's judgment.[2] In a culture in which hell and judgment have been muted or denied, we must take note that "even the demons believe—and shudder!" (James 2:19). Such an insight points us to the truth of the gospel, that "all have sinned" (Rom. 3:23) and that only through redemption in Christ is a person freed from God's judgment. Let us, then, outdo the belief of the demons and confess and worship Christ!

Whole-Bible Connections

CHRISTIAN TESTIMONY. It is likely that, when Christians hear the word "testimony," they think about a person's sharing his or her personal testimony, that is, the story of his or her conversion and faith in Christ. While that is a fine and good use, the Bible uses "testimony" more often and regularly in the sense of "witness," a legal term that serves to point to, give evidence about, or simply proclaim someone or something. This is what Jesus asks the formerly demonized man to do: "Return to your home, and declare how much God has done for you. And he went away, proclaiming throughout the whole city how much Jesus had done for him" (Luke 8:39). This theme is common in both Testaments (e.g., Ps. 71:15–18; John 15:27; 1 Pet. 3:15; 1 John 5:11). Jesus' final words before his ascension are the command to "be my witnesses" (Acts 1:8), and the biblical story shows how the people of God—those who have experienced the healing work of Christ—proclaim him "to the end of the earth."

HE GAVE THEM PERMISSION. There is no doubt that Jesus was the person in charge of this powerful encounter between himself and a man filled with many demons. The narrative magnifies this not only by the demons' "begging" Jesus to treat them mercifully (Luke 8:31) but also by Luke's description of Jesus' giving them "permission" (8:32). The entire biblical story explains that the Creator reigns over his creation and all its creatures—humans and angels alike. The demons beg and need permission because they are speaking to the one "who was seated on the throne" (Rev. 5:1). The biblical theology of the kingship of Jesus is again supported in this miracle as Jesus displays his sovereign rule over heavenly beings.

Theological Soundings

NOT MERELY FLESH AND BLOOD. From Genesis to Revelation the Bible describes the reality of such spiritual creatures as angels and demons, including Satan. In a modern culture in which demons are restricted to myths and movies, this account reminds us that we must believe in Scripture's witness to the spiritual realities and creatures beyond what we can see or fully understand. As the apostle Paul explains, our spiritual conflicts are not only "against flesh and blood, but against . . . the cosmic powers over this present darkness, against the spiritual forces of evil in the heavenly places" (Eph. 6:12). This truth does not shake us or embarrass us but directs us to rest fully and finally in the redeeming work and sovereign care of our Lord Jesus Christ.

FEAR OF GOD. The witnesses of Jesus' power over the demons are "seized with great fear" (Luke 8:37). While the Bible is well-aware that humanity will have a fear of God, the Bible also explains that, when Christians are in right relationship to God as participants in the blessing of the new covenant, they will have a proper fear of God. Such passages as Exodus 20:18–20 and Jeremiah 32:39–40 suggest that a proper fear of God is one in which a person is truly and rightly committed to God, ordering one's life under the sovereign and loving reign of God. This is a fear that induces not panic but piety and not dread but discipleship, for "The fear of the Lord is the beginning of wisdom" (Prov. 9:10).

Personal Implications

Take some time to reflect on what you have learned from your study of Luke 8:26–39 and how it might apply to your own life today. Make notes below on the personal implications for your walk with the Lord of the (1) *Gospel Glimpses*, (2) *Whole-Bible Connections*, (3) *Theological Soundings*, and (4) this passage as a whole.

1. Gospel Glimpses

2. Whole-Bible Connections

3. Theological Soundings

4. Luke 8:26–39

As You Finish This Unit . . .

Jesus is Lord over all, including the spiritual forces of evil. In light of this truth take a moment to look back through this study and reflect on the ways in which the lordship of Jesus supports and strengthens your faith. Spend some time in prayer before the Lord, reflecting on this truth.

Definitions

[1] **Demon** – An evil spirit that can inhabit a human being and cause him or her to carry out its will. Demons (fallen and corrupted angels) were created by God and are always limited by God. Jesus and his followers cast out many demons, demonstrating Jesus' superiority over them. All demons will one day be defeated along with Satan (Matt. 25:41; Rev. 20:10).

[2] **Judgment** – Any assessment of something or someone, especially a moral assessment. The Bible also speaks of a final day of judgment when Christ returns, when all those who have refused to repent will be judged (Rev. 20:12–15).

WEEK 6: JESUS CURSES THE FIG TREE

Mark 11:12–25

The Place of the Passage

The exchange of rings in a wedding ceremony is a well-known symbolic act, an act that represents something else. The giving and receiving of the rings express the covenantal commitment into which both the groom and the bride commit themselves. The act is recognized as a symbol of marriage itself. The strange miracle of Jesus' cursing the fig tree is also a symbolic act. The Gospel of Mark makes this clear by telling the miracle in two parts (Mark 11:12–14, 20–25) that surround the account of the cleansing the temple[1] like a frame (11:15–19). By intertwining the two stories in this way Mark merges them so that they form a unified message. And this message is reflected in this type of miracle, a miracle of destruction, that reflects God's judgment. As an "old creation" miracle, the cursing of the fig tree expresses God's judgment in this world—in this case regarding the religious practices of God's people. In this miracle Jesus reveals a primary purpose of his ministry and how he serves as the judge of the world.

The Big Picture

Jesus Christ is the judge of the world who purges religious profiteering and hypocritical self-gain and calls his people to repentance and faith in God.

Reflection and Discussion

Read through the complete passage for this study, Mark 11:12–25. Then review the following questions and record your responses. (For further background, see the *ESV Study Bible*, pages 1918–1919, or visit esv.org.)

The Setting (Mark 11:15–19)

Notice that this account takes place in the middle of Mark 11:12–25. How does the surrounding account of the cursing of the fig tree help us understand Jesus' actions in the temple?

Jesus' anger is directed toward those who are commodifying worship in the temple, turning a holy place into a place of business. What would be some modern-day equivalents of this in our churches or Christian organizations and activities?

Jesus still cares about his followers' having the correct posture of religious devotion. Are there any parts of your personal or public worship that you perform or are tempted to perform for personal gain?

The Miracle (Mark 11:12–14)

Sometimes the simple details of a text can teach important truths. Jesus is drawn to the fig tree because he is hungry (11:12). What does this teach us about the humanity of Jesus and his experience of life in general?

Jesus approaches the fig tree expecting fruit but then observes that it is out of season (see *ESV Study Bible* notes for 11:13–14 on page 1918). This is an enacted parable[2] wherein Jesus uses a physical item to teach a lesson. What is the theological lesson of this miracle of destruction?

What does Jesus' curse of the fig tree ("may no one ever eat fruit from you again," 11:14) teach us about how seriously we should resist hypocrisy in religious practice?

The Conclusion (Mark 11:20–25)

Shortly after Peter discovers the miracle (11:21) Jesus teaches the disciples about faith and forgiveness (11:22–25). How are these lessons from Jesus connected to the enacted parable of cursing the fig tree?

Jesus encourages his followers toward faith as a means of bearing fruit. What areas of your life currently lack faith? Whom in your life do you need to forgive? How are these words from Jesus both a warning and an encouragement?

Christians may be tempted to take verse 24 out of context and think our prayers are blank checks from God to get whatever we want. How does a Christian's faith not only allow us to make petitions to God but also provide us with guidelines and postures for our prayers?

In light of the purpose of miracles, what does this miracle teach Christians about the person of Jesus (who he is) or the work of Jesus (what he has done for us)?

Read through the following three sections on *Gospel Glimpses*, *Whole-Bible Connections*, and *Theological Soundings*. Then take time to consider the *Personal Implications* these sections have for you.

Gospel Glimpses

JESUS CLEANSES. The unique structure of this miracle connects Jesus' words against the fig tree (11:14) with his actions in the temple after his entrance into Jerusalem (11:15–19). The crowd's response to Jesus' halting the selling of pigeons in the temple is that of fear and astonishment (11:15–16, 18–19). In Romans 3:1–20 Paul reiterates the universal uncleanliness of all people, Jew and Gentile alike. This miracle invites the reader to respond in astonishment at the truth that Jesus has the authority to cleanse the unworthy areas of our hearts. Those profiting from religious devotion for personal gain are like the fig tree that will bear no fruit, but those who respond in faith (Mark 11:22) can do mighty things (11:23–24) and approach the Father confidently in prayer (11:25).

A FORGIVING FATHER. The final section of teaching concerning this miracle connects the act of faith (which produces fruit) with the practice of forgiveness. It is contradictory to be a faith-filled follower of Jesus and to live with an unforgiving heart. Because the life of the Christian is one that has been won ultimately through grace by the forgiveness of sins, forgiveness is then the default posture and practice of the believer. Jesus' teaching on forgiveness in the miracle account connects the act of forgiving with the ministry of the heavenly Father. When the believer forgives, their "Father also who is in heaven" forgives trespasses (11:25, cf. Matt. 6:14–15). Said simply, the forgiven are forgivers.

Whole-Bible Connections

THE TIME OF THE GENTILES. Jesus' cleansing of the temple regards the perverting of a place of prayer to a place of business and prosperity. The outer courts of the temple were to be a "house of prayer for all the nations" (11:17; i.e., the Gentiles). Jesus is intentionally using prophetic language in this rebuke to evoke the imagery of Isaiah 56:7. In Isaiah 56 the prophet communicates a vision of the kingdom of God in which all people, foreigners included, will have access to the covenant Lord (Yahweh). The mission of Jesus is to make a people from every tribe, language, people, and nation (Rev. 5:9–10), and this mission begins during his earthly ministry and is handed to his disciples in the Great Commission (Matt. 28:16–20).

THE FIG TREE AND ISRAEL. Jesus' selection of a fig tree is not random, although figs were a common tree in the ancient Near East. Throughout the Old Testament, specifically in the writings of the prophets, the fig tree stands as an image for the people of God (see Jer. 8:13; Hos. 9:10, 16; Joel 1:7). This enacted parable is a pronouncement of judgment on the proud and wicked religious leaders who have twisted the law of God and are actively challenging the mission and message of Jesus.

Theological Soundings

THE JUDGMENT OF GOD. In this miracle we see demonstrated Jesus' role as judge. The miracle of destruction is functionally a miracle of judgment, wherein Jesus rules over the religious leaders through an enacted parable. This parable presents a stark picture of Jesus the Lord for all of Jesus' disciples, past and present, and the role that Jesus will play as judge. Paul reflects a similar theology in 2 Corinthians 5:10: "We must all appear before the judgment seat of Christ, so that each one may receive what is due for what he has done in the body, whether good or evil."

PRAYER IN FAITH. Jesus' depiction of the undoubting faith of the Christian could easily lead a person to assume that the power of prayer is our faith. But Jesus uses hyperbolic language (e.g., moving mountains) to make his point strongly, as when a coach says to give 110 percent. But the text itself reveals two important theological qualifications. First, the faith that empowers the prayer of a Christian is "in God" (Mark 11:22). This simple phrase means that prayer is empowered not from within the Christian but by God. Faith is not the Christian's source of power but the Christian's submitted position before God. It is trusting what God alone can do. Second, the Christian can have no control of the prayer if it is "done for him" (11:23). Prayer must be an asking, not a commanding, for God alone is the one who must act and will. As Jesus similarly taught us to pray elsewhere, "your will be done" (Matt. 6:10). None of these qualifications should minimize the power of prayer; they simply serve to make our prayers acts of faith and therefore biblically faithful.

Personal Implications

Take some time to reflect on what you have learned from your study of Mark 11:12–25 and how it might apply to your own life today. Make notes below on the personal implications for your walk with the Lord of the (1) *Gospel Glimpses*, (2) *Whole-Bible Connections*, (3) *Theological Soundings*, and (4) this passage as a whole.

1. Gospel Glimpses

2. Whole-Bible Connections

3. Theological Soundings

4. Mark 11:12–25

As You Finish This Unit . . .

Jesus the just judge will always do what is right. Those who come to him in faith receive the Father's forgiveness. Reflect on this beautiful truth in your own life and respond to the Lord in prayer.

Definitions

[1] **Temple** – A place set aside as holy because of God's presence there. Solomon built the first temple of the Lord in Jerusalem to replace the portable tabernacle. This temple was later destroyed by the Babylonians, then rebuilt by Herod and destroyed again by the Romans.

[2] **Parable** – A story that uses everyday imagery and activities to communicate a spiritual truth. Jesus often taught in parables (e.g., Matthew 13).

WEEK 7: JESUS CALMS THE STORM

Mark 4:35–41

The Place of the Passage

The structure of the Gospel of Mark positions the miracle of Jesus' calming the storm within the context of Jesus' later ministry in Galilee (See *ESV Study Bible*, pages 1891–1892, 1894). Thematically, Mark includes this miracle within a section of Scripture that demonstrates Jesus' authority over nature, including miracles of exorcism (see Mark 5:1–19) and healing (5:21–43). While the miracles of exorcism and healing are categorically different in this study (see miracles of healing in Weeks 4–5), they are thematically similar in the simple fact that Jesus demonstrates power over the physical creation (both nature and people). This miracle itself is a miracle of dominion, a demonstration of God's power over his created universe. While this miracle of calming the storm fits within the context of the economy of old creation, other miracles in this category of dominion preview life in God's new creation (see Week 8: Jesus Walks on Water). In this miracle Jesus reveals a crucial purpose of his ministry and how he intends to rule over our world as the Lord of all creation.

The Big Picture

Jesus Christ demonstrates his authority over creation as he rescues the disciples from a storm by calming the winds and the sea.

Reflection and Discussion

Read through the complete passage for this study, Mark 4:35–41. Then review the following questions and record your responses. (For further background, see the *ESV Study Bible*, page 1901, or visit esv.org.)

The Setting (Mark 4:35–38)

A great windstorm rises and threatens the boat that Jesus and his disciples are using. How does the narrative show the seriousness of the situation? Have you ever been in a physically threating situation? How did you respond?

The contrast between the raging storm and the resting Jesus is stark. What does this teach us about the humanity of Jesus and his disposition in the face of threats? What does the disciples' rebuke of Jesus reveal about their handling of the storm?

Of what Old Testament narrative does this account remind you? How does Jesus' response differ from that of the Old Testament prophet? What does this teach us about Jesus?

The Miracle (Mark 4:39)

Jesus calms the storm with words of rebuke. What does this teach about the power and authority of Jesus? Since Jesus is the creator of all things (John 1:3), how does his lordship over all things give you confidence and hope?

There is no struggle or delay when Jesus commands the wind and sea to be still. How does this instruct us to trust Jesus with our physical lives and not just our spiritual lives?

The Conclusion (Mark 4:40–41)

The disciple's response to Jesus' command over the wind and the storm is not surprising. What does their response reveal about the human heart, and what does Jesus' response teach us about faith in difficult moments? Are there any circumstances in your life concerning which Jesus is exhorting you to express faith?

What is the significance of the question the disciples propose in response to Jesus' rebuke, "Who then is this, that even the wind and the sea obey him" (Mark 4:41)? What is the correct answer to their question?

In light of the purpose of miracles, what does this miracle teach Christians about the person of Jesus (who he is) or the work of Jesus (what he has done for us)?

Read through the following three sections on *Gospel Glimpses*, *Whole-Bible Connections*, and *Theological Soundings*. Then take time to consider the *Personal Implications* these sections have for you.

Gospel Glimpses

JESUS AND THE STORM. There is a simple truth present in this passage that comforts the believer: when the disciples are in danger and scared, Jesus is present with them. The full picture of the gospel proclaims Jesus not only as Redeemer but also as Creator (Heb. 1:1–2). This means that, even though life's trials are not promised to go away, comfort can be found in Jesus, the one who dwells in the storm that his disciples are facing and who controls the strong wind and the raging sea. A product of this miracle of dominion is believers who are steadfast in suffering.

FAITH AND FEAR. The response of the disciples is understandable, given the terrifying circumstances. Who wouldn't respond to this miracle with a sense of awe and trembling? Often, the image of Jesus is that of the servant who is meek and mild. While this is a true portrait, it is not the whole story. To see Jesus rightly is to see him as one with complete, sovereign control over his whole creation. Creation bends the knee to our Lord, the Creator. This biblical truth should engender reverent fear[1] in the lives of believers, alongside a confident certainty and hope in all circumstances, even in storms.

Whole-Bible Connections

THE BETTER JONAH. Mark's account of the calming of the storm includes the detail of Jesus' being asleep on a cushion (Mark 4:28). While not explicitly stated, the reader is reminded of another prophet asleep on a boat: Jonah (see Jonah 1:5). By contrast, while Jonah attempts to flee the will of God and ends up succumbing to the forces of nature, Jesus, in complete alignment with the heavenly Father, pronounces peace over the storm. Jesus' obedience to the will of God will eventually lead him to the cross, as he is the better Jonah—not only a prophet to the nations but the Savior of the nations.

JESUS THE CREATOR. Jesus speaks peace into the storm, and the wind and the seas obey. An adjacent image in the story of God's Word is the image of a formless earth with darkness over the face of the deep (Gen. 1:1). In the creation account the Creator God speaks over creation and brings about structure, life, and purpose. As God uses words as a means of creating *ex nihilo* (see *ESV Study Bible* notes on page 49), creation is ordered and declared good. Hebrews 1:2 makes it clear that Jesus Christ is indeed "the heir of all things, through whom also [God] created the world." In a fallen world Creator Jesus speaks over creation and brings about peace. Jesus is both our Savior and our Creator.

Theological Soundings

THE HUMANITY OF JESUS. When the storm begins, Jesus can be found asleep on the boat, lying on a cushion (Mark 4:38). This seemingly insignificant detail is not to be ignored. Jesus is burdened by the ministry and the call to follow God, and as a man he needs rest. On display in this text is the fullness of Christ's humanity. Some understandings of Jesus, while focusing on his power and authority, accidentally underappreciate his true humanity. Jesus felt the full force of exhaustion, and Jesus needed rest. This minor detail in the miracle account helps believers relate to Jesus as our sympathizing Great High Priest (Heb. 4:14–16).

THE SOVEREIGNTY OF GOD. There is something powerful about this teacher! Jesus demonstrates creational dominion in this miracle because he is indeed the Creator himself. Present in this reality is the truth of his sovereignty.[2] His control over the winds and the seas extends into our lives and brings comfort in times of trial. While the sovereignty of God can often be a debated topic of theological extrapolation and overspeculation, in this miracle text it is a pastoral gift to those scared by life's storms.

CONTRA-GNOSTICISM. A heresy present throughout much of church history is that of Gnosticism. Gnosticism teaches that true humanity resides in the soul alone. The physicality of creation is viewed through a purely negative lens, as something that needs to be disdained. Believers can easily fall victim to this belief system when they adopt escapist views of eschatology (the doctrine of the end times). Jesus' calming of the storm reminds the believer that the peace extended to believers through the forgiveness of sins is only part of the story. Jesus' creational might and mercy will be demonstrated in all of creation, as the war-torn creation groans for renewal and peace (Rom. 8:22–23).

Personal Implications

Take some time to reflect on what you have learned from your study of Mark 4:35–41 and how it might apply to your own life today. Make notes below on the personal implications for your walk with the Lord of the (1) *Gospel Glimpses*, (2) *Whole-Bible Connections*, (3) *Theological Soundings*, and (4) this passage as a whole.

1. Gospel Glimpses

2. Whole-Bible Connections

3. Theological Soundings

4. Mark 4:35–41

As You Finish This Unit . . .

Jesus calms the storms and demonstrates his power as sovereign Creator. Reflect on how this truth has comforted you during the trials of your life, and respond in prayer.

Definitions

[1] **Fear** – Has both godly and ungodly meanings in the Bible, depending on the context. Fear of the Lord is a godly, wise fear that demonstrates awe and reverence for the all-powerful God (Prov. 1:7). Conversely, Jesus taught his disciples not to fear people or situations in a way that shows a lack of trust in God's protection (Matt. 10:26–31).

[2] **Sovereignty** – Supreme and independent power and authority. Sovereignty over all things is a distinctive attribute of God (1 Tim. 6:15–16). He directs all things to carry out his purposes (Rom. 8:28–29).

WEEK 8: JESUS WALKS ON WATER

Matthew 14:22–33

The Place of the Passage

The miracle of Jesus' walking on water is another instance of a miracle of dominion. In this miracle Jesus reveals his unique relationship to nature and thus the proper relationship between the Creator and his creation. If the calming of the storm displayed the way in which Jesus ministers authoritatively over creation for the good of our world, then this miracle displays Jesus' harmonious relationship to creation that he ministerially provides for the world to come. Jesus' defiance of the physical properties of water and the limitations of gravity project the nature of human life in the new creation. As the encounter between Jesus and Peter will show, this reality of the new creation, while not yet fully here, has already begun. This miracle of dominion not only leaves believers with hope amid this present world and its toil but also gives us a glimpse into life in the glory of the new creation. In this miracle Jesus reveals a crucial purpose of his ministry and how the lordship of Jesus offers a foretaste of the glorious new life God promises to his people and his creation.

The Big Picture

Jesus is the Lord of his creation, whose operations in this world serve as a witness to the glories of the world to come.

Reflection and Discussion

Read through the complete passage for this study, Matthew 14:22–33. Then review the following questions and record your responses. (For further background, see the *ESV Study Bible*, pages 1851–1852, or visit esv.org.)

The Setting (Matthew 14:22–24)

The introduction to the miracle might seem odd: Jesus sends his disciples[1] ahead before praying alone, and the waves slow the boat as Jesus catches up on foot—by walking on the water! But how does this strangeness magnify Jesus' control over all the time-and-space elements of creation?

Jesus is not on the boat with the disciples, because he is alone on the mountain praying (14:23). What is the significance of Jesus' praying? What does his habit of prayer, especially alone at times (cf. Matt. 14:13; Mark 1:35; Luke 5:16; 6:12), model for the prayer life of Christians?

The Miracle (Matthew 14:25–30)

The image is shocking: Jesus comes to his disciples in the boat by "walking on the sea" (14:25). What is this defiance of nature intended to communicate to Jesus' disciples—and us—about the way in which Jesus rules over and in his creation?

Do the responses of the disciples surprise you in any way? How is fear a fitting response of the Christian to God, and what does reverent fear look like (see Prov. 9:10)?

Jesus comforts the terrified disciples by presenting himself to them. How does Jesus comfort us with his presence today? In what ways have you experienced the ministry of Christ in your life?

Peter walks on the water too, even if only briefly (Matt. 14:28–30). How does this short-lived miracle reflect the inbreaking of the new creation Jesus represents and will one day bring? What other areas of the Christian life reflect the inbreaking of the new creation?

The Conclusion (Matthew 14:31–33)

Jesus saves Peter from sinking into the sea but also issues him a rebuke. What is Jesus' rebuke of Peter intended to teach him? In what ways do we similarly doubt or lack faith, for which Jesus would rebuke us?

The conclusion of this miracle leads to the calming of the sea, followed by the disciples' worship of Jesus (15:32–33). Is worship the automatic response of your heart when you see the work of God in your life? Why or why not?

In light of the purpose of miracles, what does this miracle teach Christians about the person of Jesus (who he is) or the work of Jesus (what he has done for us)?

Read through the following three sections on *Gospel Glimpses*, *Whole-Bible Connections*, and *Theological Soundings*. Then take time to consider the *Personal Implications* these sections have for you.

Gospel Glimpses

THE COMMANDS OF JESUS. A unique component of this miracle is Peter's participation in it. Amazed at the sight of Jesus on the water, Peter asks Jesus to command him to walk on water (Matt. 14:28). At the command of Jesus, Peter participates in the miracle, even if only for a few moments. While this event is not prescriptive to the life of believers, there are still lessons to learn about discipleship. The commands of the Lord Jesus are the assignments of his disciples. Moreover, just as Jesus' miracles are signs that point people to him, so also are Jesus' disciples commanded to "make disciples of all nations" (Matt. 28:19). At the command of Jesus all God's people respond in obedience.

THE SON OF GOD. The climax of this miracle event is worship. When Peter and Jesus return to the boat and the sea calms, the disciples respond in praise, "Truly you are the Son of God" (Matt. 14:33). This is the truth the disciples—and we as readers—are supposed to see and believe. As we are witnesses of this "sign," Jesus' rebuke is directed at us as well: "O you of little faith, why did you doubt?" (14:31). Do not doubt but believe in the Son of God.

Whole-Bible Connections

IT IS I AM. At first appearance the disciples think Jesus might be a ghost approaching the boat. His response in verse 27 is meant to comfort them: "Take heart; it is I." While this statement might not seem too special in English, Jesus chooses these words intentionally. The original construction is identical to the one used in Exodus 3, where God speaks of himself as "I am" (Ex. 3:14). In this miracle Jesus *shows* that he is God (he controls the wind and waves), and he *says* so as well! The words of Jesus are as shocking as the walking on water. The waves of the sea are a stroll in a park for the "I Am."

DO NOT BE AFRAID. The second half of Jesus' comforting statement to the scared disciples is the exhortation not to be afraid. While fear is a common experience of the disciples after Jesus performs a miracle, a common response from Jesus is to comfort them. In fact a theme throughout the Bible is the exhortation to fear not, which appears frequently in the Old Testament (e.g., Deut. 31:8; Josh. 1:9) and the New Testament (1 Pet. 3:6; 1 John 4:18). While the believer is called to fear God as an act of love and worship, this is uniquely different from worldly fears that are often experienced by believers and nonbelievers alike. This distinction is taught by Jesus not only in his care for the disciples in this miracle itself but in his teaching elsewhere, such as, "Do not fear those who kill the body but cannot kill the soul. Rather fear him who can destroy both soul and body in hell" (Matt. 10:28).

Theological Soundings

JESUS PRAYS. The setting of the miracle positions Jesus away from the disciples as he desires time to pray to the Father. This intercession[2] is a preview of the ministry currently being accomplished by the resurrected and ascended Son of God. As Jesus prayed then, so he prays now for his church. Operating in the office of high priest, Jesus holds this office permanently and thus "is able to save the uttermost those who draw near to God through him, since he always lives to make intercession for them" (Heb. 7:25). Christ's intercession is a gift to the church and a testimony to the power of prayer in the lives of believers.

ALREADY AND NOT YET. This miracle involves not only Jesus but Peter, who shares in this miraculous act. But, while Peter also walks on the water, he quickly begins to sink until he touches the hand of Jesus. As a miracle of dominion, the walking on water is a sign of the world to come, the glories of the new creation. This is where Peter's participation in the miracle is so important, for it reflects the inbreaking or beginning of the world to come in the world that is now. Theologians refer to this reality as the "already and not yet." The death, resurrection, and ascension of Jesus "already" give the Christian aspects of the new creation (e.g., freedom from sin and death, the gift of the Holy Spirit), but the fullness of the new creation is "not yet" upon us. It is still to come. In this miracle Peter shows us this already-and-not-yet reality. He tastes the water-walking with Jesus for a moment but cannot sustain apart from holding his hand. Even as we live in this tension, we too now "walk by faith, not by sight" (2 Cor. 5:7). But, as the old hymn prays, "And Lord, haste the day when my faith shall be sight."

Personal Implications

Take some time to reflect on what you have learned from your study of Matthew 14:22–33 and how it might apply to your own life today. Make notes below on the personal implications for your walk with the Lord of the (1) *Gospel Glimpses*, (2) *Whole-Bible Connections*, (3) *Theological Soundings*, and (4) this passage as a whole.

1. Gospel Glimpses

2. Whole-Bible Connections

3. Theological Soundings

4. Matthew 14:22–33

As You Finish This Unit . . .

Reflect on the challenging moments of your life and how Jesus has met you in them. Respond to this grace by proclaiming in prayer, "Truly you are the Son of God."

Definitions

[1] **Disciple** – Any person who submits to the teachings of another. In the New Testament it refers to those who submitted themselves to the teaching of Jesus, especially those who traveled with him during his earthly ministry.

[2] **Intercession** – Appealing to one person on behalf of another. Often used with reference to prayer.

Week 9: Jesus Reveals His Glory

Matthew 17:1–13

The Place of the Passage

The transfiguration[1] is a climactic moment in the story of Scripture and specifically the ministry of Jesus. It is a significant moment in the life of Jesus when he transfigures or transforms before his disciples so that they experience in the flesh the glory of God made known in Jesus Christ. It is a moment in which the disciples share the light of Jesus, a light that will one day fill all the earth: "The city has no need of sun or moon to shine on it, for the glory of God gives it light, and its lamp is the Lamb" (Rev. 21:23). This is a preview or trailer for the reality of the new creation and a unique revelation by which Christians are given true hope. The transfiguration reveals that Christ unites the living and the dead, the old and new covenants, and even the age to come so that the transformation of the Christian is guaranteed (see 2 Cor. 3:18). For this reason this miracle is categorized as a miracle of glorification, because it is a revelation of the true majesty and perfection of Jesus. The transfiguration is intimately connected to the cross; together the two declare that light defeats darkness and that Jesus' humiliation is also his exaltation (John 12:32–33). This category of miracle, glorification, rests in the economy of the new creation, as its purpose is connected to the revelation of truths about the life to come.

The Big Picture

Jesus is the glorious Son of God, and the revelation of his glory is a present hope and a future reality.

Reflection and Discussion

Read through the complete passage for this study, Matthew 17:1–13. Then review the following questions and record your responses. (For further background, see the *ESV Study Bible*, pages 1856–1857, or visit esv.org.)

The Setting (Matthew 17:1)

Jesus waits six days before taking the disciples up the mountain (Matt. 17:1). What could be the potential significance of both the six days and the mountain? (Hint: read Exodus 24:16.)

Jesus takes Peter, James, and John with him up the mountain. What could be potential reasons that Jesus does not take all the disciples?

While the actual identity of the mountain that the disciples climb is debated (see *ESV Study Bible* note on 17:1, page 1856), what does the act of ascending to high places signify?

The Miracle (Matthew 17:2–8)

What would the transfigured Jesus have look liked to the human eye or have been like to experience in person? What would the experience communicate about Jesus?

Why do Moses and Elijah appear next to Jesus? (Hint: see *The ESV Study Bible* note on 17:3, page 1856.)

What is misguided about Peter's response to the miracle (see 17:4)?

What is the significance of the pronouncement from the heavens and the disappearance of the two Old Testament leaders (17:5–8)? What does this scene, and especially the statement from the Father, teach us about Jesus?

The Conclusion (Matthew 17:9–13)

After the completion of the miracle, Jesus charges the disciples not to share with others the vision they have witnessed until the resurrection (17:9). What would be the purpose of this secrecy, and what does it teach us about the importance of the resurrection?

The disciples show their confusion and ask Jesus a question about Elijah. How does Jesus' answer show a fulfillment of the prophecy of Malachi 4:4–6? What does this teach us about the unified plan of God from the Old Testament to the New Testament, as well as the climactic role of Jesus?

In light of the purpose of miracles, what does this miracle teach Christians about the person of Jesus (who he is) or the work of Jesus (what he has done for us)?

Read through the following three sections on *Gospel Glimpses*, *Whole-Bible Connections*, and *Theological Soundings*. Then take time to consider the *Personal Implications* these sections have for you.

Gospel Glimpses

THE GLORY OF JESUS. Peter, James, and John are given a sneak peek of the majesty of Jesus. While the Son must still be tried, handed over to the Romans, and crucified, this preview miracle teaches believers that the gospel is fundamentally connected to the glorification of the Son. The words from the Father at Jesus' baptism are repeated on the mountain: "This is my beloved Son, with whom I am well pleased" (Matt. 3:17). Any claim to Christianity that seeks to take glory away from the Son and redirect to self is a deviation and misappreciation of the gospel (see Col. 1:15–23).

THE SON MUST RISE. Jesus often seeks to conceal the results of his ministry (healings, exorcisms, etc.) by charging the recipient with secrecy (Matt. 8:4; cf. 9:30; 12:16; 16:20). After coming down the mountain he delivers a similar charge to the three disciples with him. In this case, however, Jesus offers a bit more explanation by specifying that any information must be delayed until after the resurrection: "Tell no one the vision, until the Son of Man is raised from the dead" (Matt. 17:9). As Jesus has predicted his death, that death and his subsequent resurrection lend context to Jesus' secretive nature. The resurrection of Christ is not only the central point of the story but the interpretive key to make sense of the whole. The resurrection, which is another miracle of glorification, is the final revelatory statement of Jesus by which he declares the reality of the glory revealed only partially in the transfiguration.

Whole-Bible Connections

THE LAW AND THE PROPHETS. A unique component of this miracle is the appearance of Moses and Elijah. While there is much scholarly debate concerning their purpose in the miracle, a majority consensus addresses their distinct but cooperative roles in communicating what is true about Jesus: Both the law of God (given by Moses) and the prophetic announcement of the coming Messiah (revealed by Elijah) reach their fulfilled climax in the person and work of Jesus Christ. The transfiguration connects the old covenant (testament) to the new covenant (testament), uniting the whole story of Scripture and the progressive revelation of God in the world to the person and work of Jesus Christ.

THE TIME OF ELIJAH. The appearance of Elijah on the mountain spurs a question from the disciples concerning the prophetic expectation of his arrival. In Malachi 4:4–6, the last verses of our Old Testament, the waiting world is given a prophetic picture of the day of the Lord.[2] Before this "great and awesome day," a major sign given by the Old Testament is the arrival of the prophet Elijah. While Elijah himself was spared from death (2 Kings 2), his return marks the beginning of the turning point in human history. But his return is not as straightforward as the disciples expect, as Jesus connects this prophecy with the life and ministry of John the Baptist. As the four Gospels reveal, John prepares the way for Jesus, and thus for the great day of the Lord (see *ESV Study Bible* notes on Mal. 4:4–6, pages 1779–1780).

Theological Soundings

GLORIFICATION. While this miracle is a snapshot or a vision of the glorious realities of the new creation, the message of this miracle extends through Christ to believers, who have been united to him by faith. The life of faith is a life of growth toward Jesus in obedience to his word and love of neighbor. This process in Christian theology is called sanctification. The finality of this growth, completed at the death of the believer, is called glorification. As Christ is glorified, so one day we will be also. The apostle Paul in 2 Corinthians 3:18 explains this process: "We all, with unveiled face, beholding the glory of the Lord, are being transformed into the same image from one degree of glory to another." This transformation will be completed when Christ returns.

JESUS ONLY. The reverent fear of the disciples on the mountain leads to the exhortation from Jesus, "Rise, and have no fear" (Matt. 17:7). When the disciples rise up and look to their Lord, they see only him. Without explanation Elijah and Moses have disappeared, and they see "no one but Jesus only." The shift from three men on the mountain to the one proclaims the central claim of Christianity, that a person can see the glory of God only through the Son of God, Jesus Christ. Only through Jesus' person and his work—his death, resurrection, and ascension—can the believer ascend "the mountain" of the Lord. This truth is a wonderful and exclusive truth. Not only can no one attain righteousness through the law (Romans 2), but no one can attain justification[3] through any other source (religion) ever conceived or created either. It is through Jesus, and only Jesus, that a person can be saved!

Personal Implications

Take some time to reflect on what you have learned from your study of Matthew 17:1–13 and how it might apply to your own life today. Make notes below on the personal implications for your walk with the Lord of the (1) *Gospel Glimpses*, (2) *Whole-Bible Connections*, (3) *Theological Soundings*, and (4) this passage as a whole.

1. Gospel Glimpses

2. Whole-Bible Connections

3. Theological Soundings

4. Matthew 17:1–13

As You Finish This Unit . . .

God's Word gives you an insider vision of Jesus in his true glory! Reflect on what this means for your life and respond in prayer.

Definitions

[1] **Transfiguration** – An event in the life of Jesus Christ in which his physical appearance was transfigured, that is, changed to reflect his heavenly glory.

[2] **Day of the Lord** – According to the Old Testament prophets, God would come at the end of history, judging his enemies and restoring his people. This was referred to throughout the Old Testament as the "day of the Lord" (e.g., Isa. 13:9; Joel 1–3; Zechariah 12–14; Mal. 4:5). Also, any day on which God took action in judgment might be called a "day of the Lord" (e.g., Amos 5:15–20).

[3] **Justification** – The act of God's grace in bringing sinners into a new covenant relationship with himself through the forgiveness of sins, and in counting them as righteous before him through their faith in Christ alone (Rom. 3:20–26).

Week 10: Jesus Raises the Dead

John 11:1–57

The Place of the Passage

The miracles of Jesus display God's ministry in a sin-filled, broken world. The miracles of fertility, healing, destruction, and dominion all reflect the redeeming work of God in his creation with operations fitting the old creation, returning aspects of the physical world to its original (even if still broken) state. This miracle is the first of a smaller set of Jesus' miracles that display operations fitting the coming world, as Jesus redeems aspects of the physical world in alignment with the new creation. In the biblical story the ultimate opponent of life is death. As the apostle Paul writes, "The last enemy to be destroyed is death" (1 Cor. 15:26). Although the final consequence of sin in the old creation is death, the end of a created life (Rom. 6:23), in the new creation "death shall be no more" (Rev. 21:4).

This perspective is essential to seeing properly the significance of the miracle of Jesus in John 11, the raising of Lazarus. At a funeral for a friend, Jesus declares himself to be the one who is making all things new. This is a miracle of reversal (i.e., "renewal"), which means it announces the coming renewal of all things, the new creation. In this miracle Jesus reveals the primary purpose of his ministry and how he intends to redeem his creation from its greatest enemy: death.

The Big Picture

Jesus is the resurrection and the life, the one who has defeated death in preparation for the life of the world to come.

Reflection and Discussion

Read through the complete passage for this study, John 11:1–57. Then review the following questions and record your responses. (For further background, see the *ESV Study Bible*, pages 2045–2047, or visit esv.org.)

The Setting (John 11:1–43)

When Jesus heard that Lazarus was ill, he said that the illness was "for the glory of God, so that the Son of God may be glorified through it" (John 11:4). How does this miracle display God's glory? How might God use our struggles and brokenness for his glory?

Why does Jesus refer to Lazarus' death as "sleep" (see 11:11–15), and what does this teach Christians about the nature of new life that Jesus provides?

Based upon her comment in verse 24, Martha seems to have a correct view of eschatology (the doctrine of "last things"), but Jesus focuses her thinking and expectation onto himself (11:25). What does Jesus mean when he says that he is "the resurrection and the life" and that the person who believes in him "though he die, yet shall he live" (11:25)?

What is the significance of Jesus' weeping at a graveside, especially when he is about to raise Lazarus from the dead (11:35)?

The Miracle (John 11:38–44)

What does Jesus' prayer to his Father before the raising of Lazarus teach us about this miracle, especially regarding the purpose of Jesus' ministry (11:41–42)?

How is Jesus' command to Lazarus to rise and come out of the tomb a new creation act, especially when compared to God's speaking creation into existence (e.g., the multiple uses of "and God said" in Genesis 1)?

Jewish burials required the corpse to be wrapped tightly with many pounds of linen and materials (e.g., a mummy). Why does John go into detail about how the resurrected Lazarus came out of the tomb bound in linens from head to toe and needing to be released (John 11:44)? How is the scene both comical and insightful?

The Conclusion (John 11:45–57)

Why does this miracle get such mixed reactions (11:45–46), and how could the religious authorities declare it to be a sign (11:47) and yet not respond in faith? How might this same response to Jesus occur today?

In light of the purpose of miracles, what does this miracle teach Christians about the person of Jesus (who he is) or the work of Jesus (what he has done for us)?

Read through the following three sections on *Gospel Glimpses*, *Whole-Bible Connections*, and *Theological Soundings*. Then take time to consider the *Personal Implications* these sections have for you.

Gospel Glimpses

THIS ILLNESS DOES NOT LEAD TO DEATH. Jesus receives the news about the serious illness of his friend Lazarus without panic or concern. When he hears the news, he responds by saying, "This illness does not lead to death. It is for the glory of God" (11:4). Behind Jesus' statement is a core truth of the gospel: for the Christian, death is defeated. Christ's resurrection is the "firstfruits" of our own future resurrection (1 Cor 15:20), with death as the "last enemy to be destroyed" (1 Cor. 15:26). Jesus explains this further to Martha in John 11:25: "Whoever believes in me, though he die, yet shall he live." The seemingly paradoxical nature of that statement reflects the radical inbreaking of eternal life into a world of death. This is the good news that the church preaches and, even more, that the Christian lives.

JESUS LOVED. Every Christian knows John 3:16, which describes God's love for the world. This truth is one of the most powerful statements in all Scripture of who God is and how blessed we are. In this account of Lazarus, however, God's love is made more personal. The narrator reveals Jesus' response to the man who was seriously sick and to his family: "Jesus loved Martha and her sister and Lazarus" (11:5). This statement is true for this family, but it is also true for every Christian in God's family. God's love of the world finds personal (and sacrificial) expression through the person of Jesus. If you believe in him, the amazing grace of the gospel is that Jesus loves you!

Whole-Bible Connections

FALLEN ASLEEP. In verses 11–15 Jesus and his disciples define "sleep" in very different ways. Jesus speaks of Lazarus' death as "sleep," but the disciples assume he is referring to taking a nap. The confusion surrounding this one word is the point: in the presence of Jesus death is redefined! In the New Testament "sleep" is used more than three times as often to refer to death as to physical sleep. While this use of "sleep" is not original to Scripture, it was the Bible that cemented this understanding of death in light of Christ. For the one who is the resurrection and the life (11:25) death is described best as sleeping, since he has authority over both life and death (5:22–29). This helps explains Paul's encouragement that Christian grief for those who have died is not like those "who have no hope" (1 Thess. 4:13), for death is altogether redefined in the presence of the resurrection and the life.

THE RESURRECTION AND THE LIFE. When Jesus refers to himself as the resurrection and the life, he is combining two biblical truths that usually point in different directions. "Resurrection" is generally applied to the future in Scripture, whereas "life" is generally applied to the present, or even to the past in regard to one's origins. The combination of these terms in reference to Jesus creates a powerful overlap of biblical thinking. This means that the present, for example, is safely wrapped in the comfort, certainty, and security of the perfect future of God's gracious providence. But that which secures the present to the future is Jesus, the one who not merely provides resurrection and life but *is* the resurrection and the life. Because of Jesus, then, the Christian's future hope is an already-but-not-yet present reality, an inaugurated eschatology.[1] This gives purpose and provision of the new creation to every present moment.

Theological Soundings

JESUS WEPT. When our Lord arrived at the tomb of his friend Lazarus, the narrator describes his reaction: "Jesus wept" (John 11:35). This is one of three descriptions of the emotional response of Jesus in this miracle account. This description is a remarkable insight into the humanity of Jesus. Jesus, the second person of the Trinity, has entered into his creation, becoming like the creatures he created, and ministers among them. Jesus had to become "like his brothers in every respect" (Heb. 2:17), so that he could properly and pastorally minister to us and then redeem us and intercede for us. The doctrine of the humanity of Jesus can be difficult to reconcile with equally important doctrine of the divinity of Jesus, but it is important to understand properly the ministry of Jesus. Jesus truly and personally can relate to our sadness and suffering, for he has experienced it with us.

FATHER, I THANK YOU THAT YOU HAVE HEARD ME. This miracle provides a helpful perspective from which to understand the divine relations within the Trinity,[2] specifically between God the Father and God the Son. Before commanding Lazarus to rise, Jesus prays to his Father and thanks him for hearing his prayer (likely an earlier prayer—maybe even a prayer spoken privately amid his earlier-described grief). The spoken prayer of the Son reviews the union that exists between the Father and the Son and the mission they share. The Father sent the Son into the world and empowered the Son, even as the Son does the work assigned to him by the Father—and all in the power and presence of the Holy Spirit. In the least this teaches Christians that the work of Jesus is the work of the Trinitarian God. It should also comfort the Christian, knowing that, just as the Son interceded on behalf of Lazarus to the Father, so also does he intercede for all Christians (Heb. 7:25).

Personal Implications

Take some time to reflect on what you have learned from your study of John 11:1–57 and how it might apply to your own life today. Make notes below on the personal implications for your walk with the Lord of the (1) *Gospel Glimpses*, (2) *Whole-Bible Connections*, (3) *Theological Soundings*, and (4) this passage as a whole.

1. Gospel Glimpses

2. Whole-Bible Connections

3. Theological Soundings

4. John 11:1–57

As You Finish This Unit . . .

Jesus is the resurrection and the life. Take some to reflect on the importance of this biblical truth, especially as you think of ways this truth applies to those facing the reality of death.

Definitions

[1] **Inaugurated eschatology** – "Eschatology" refers to "last things" and generally refers to what will happen at the end of all things when Jesus comes a second time. But the New Testament teaches that with the first coming of Christ the final age or latter days were launched. We are those "on whom the end of the ages has come" (1 Cor. 10:11). The "eschaton," the final age, has dawned in Jesus. This is what is also referred to as the "already / not yet" of biblical theology.

[2] **Trinity** – The Godhead as it exists in three distinct persons: Father, Son, and Holy Spirit. There is one God, yet he is three persons; there are not three Gods, nor do the three persons merely represent different aspects or modes of a single God. While the term Trinity is not found in the Bible, the concept is repeatedly assumed and affirmed by the writers of Scripture (e.g., Matt. 28:19; Luke 1:35; 3:22; Gal. 4:6; 2 Thess. 2:13–14; Heb. 10:29).

Week 11: Jesus Rises from the Dead

John 20:1–18

The Place of the Passage

One might assume that the raising of Lazarus and the resurrection of Jesus are equally symbolic of the coming world, both serving as signs of the new creation. However, a crucial distinction between them highlights the breaking in of the new creation into the old.

Using C. S. Lewis's terminology, we can say that Lazarus' rising was an "unmaking," while Jesus' resurrection was a "remaking." Lazarus was brought back to his former life within the old creation, destined to die again. In stark contrast, Jesus was raised into a new and glorious mode of existence—one that had never before existed. If Lazarus' miracle foreshadowed the new creation, Jesus' resurrection inaugurated it: "Each in his own order: Christ the firstfruits, then at his coming those who belong to Christ" (1 Cor. 15:23).

While Lazarus returned to a perishable body, Jesus was raised into an imperishable form—he "put on immortality" (1 Cor. 15:53). This means that Jesus' resurrection shifts the biblical narrative from the old creation to the new. Understanding this distinction is key to grasping the significance of Jesus' resurrection in John 20. In a garden scene that echoes Eden, Jesus is revealed as the "last Adam," who "became a life-giving spirit" (1 Cor. 15:45). This is not merely a return from the dead but a miracle of glorification—a sign from the coming world and the first flower of the new creation's spring. Through this event Jesus unveils the central purpose of his ministry: to establish the new creation through his own resurrected body.

The Big Picture

The resurrection of Jesus is the defeat of sin and death, the return of the gardener to reclaim his garden, and the declaration that the renewal of creation has begun.

Reflection and Discussion

Read through the complete passage for this study, John 20:1–18. Then review the following questions and record your responses. (For further background, see the *ESV Study Bible*, pages 2068–2070, or visit esv.org.)

The Setting (John 20:1–4)

This miracle account includes a great deal of symbolism from the Genesis creation account, beginning with the remark that the resurrection occurred "on the first day of the week," that is, Sunday (John 20:1). How might this "new week" symbolize a new era (new creation)? How do you think the occurrence of Jesus' resurrection on Sunday gave biblical warrant for changing the day of "the Sabbath,"[1] when the people of God gathered for worship and for rest from their worldly labors?

Why do you think Mary did not look into the tomb but ran to get the disciples, and why does the narrator describe the foot race between Peter and the other disciple (20:2–4)?

The Miracle (John 20:5–10)

The resurrection is the only miracle in John in which Jesus is the recipient and not the agent (see Acts 2:24; Gal. 1:1; 1 Pet. 3:18), even if he is involved in his own resurrection (John 2:19, 10:18). Why is this significant? What does it teach us?

Jesus' resurrection is a bodily resurrection! How does the fact that the miracle involves the body of Jesus (not just his spirit or soul) magnify the significance of this miracle? Why does this matter for our own hope of life after death, and also for how we proclaim the gospel (read 1 John 1:1–4)?

John describes in detail the linens and face cloth wrapped initially around Jesus' dead body. What is the significance of these details, especially the remark that the face cloth was folded as though to be used later for another person (John 20:6–7)?

How might it be significant that the other disciple "saw and believed" in the resurrection (20:8), and how would the disciples later understand from Scripture (the Old Testament) that Jesus "must rise from the dead" (20:9)? Where in the Old Testament might we find ideas of, images of, or allusions to the resurrection from the dead?

The Conclusion (John 20:11–18)

It is quite possible that John's detailed description of the angels' sitting on the bench where Jesus had been laid is intended to signify the angels at the two ends of the mercy seat on the ark of the covenant (20:12; see Ex. 25:18–19). If so, how does this communicate both that Jesus is the once-for-all sacrifice for God's people and that this offering was performed not in the temple but in a tomb?

Mary misidentifies Jesus as the gardener (John 20:15), but how is she also correct? How is Jesus like the original gardener, Adam in the garden of Eden (see Rom. 5:12–17)?

What was wrong with Mary's touching Jesus (20:17), and how does Jesus' response to her depict the already-but-not-yet reality of the new creation? How does this verse also magnify the importance of the ascension[2] of Jesus?

In light of the purpose of miracles, what does this miracle teach Christians about the person of Jesus (who he is) or the work of Jesus (what he has done for us)?

Read through the following three sections on *Gospel Glimpses*, *Whole-Bible Connections*, and *Theological Soundings*. Then take time to consider the *Personal Implications* these sections have for you.

Gospel Glimpses

THE ARK OF THE NEW COVENANT. The carefully crafted symbolism of the angels and their intentional placement on the seat where Jesus had been raised seems to borrow from the ark of the covenant in the Old Testament (Ex. 25:18–19). If the ark of the covenant, and the place between the angels, was the mercy seat, how much more so is Jesus' empty tomb! With symbols and images that strain the theological imagination God has made this tomb his new Most Holy Place and this corpse seat his new mercy seat, all in a way that presents this garden tomb as the ark of the new covenant. The resurrection of Jesus declares once and for all that the Lord Jesus Christ is now present with and powerful enough to save his people.

THE FACT OF THE EMPTY TOMB. The narrative goes to great lengths to testify to the fact of the empty tomb. The detail with which John explains the empty and forsaken grave linens makes the resurrection of Jesus emphatically clear. The message of the passage is simple: "Christ is risen!" The church has used this greeting for centuries. It serves as a declaration that the work of Jesus has been accomplished and fulfilled, and it serves as a promise that the restoration of all things has now been guaranteed—and even begun. The resurrection of Jesus is the foundation of the Christian faith. Because the tomb was empty, all those who believe in Jesus shall be resurrected to eternal life.

Whole-Bible Connections

THE TESTIMONY OF SCRIPTURE. It is right for Christians to utilize evidence from our created world to support the truthfulness and the fact of the resurrection of Jesus, but we must also acknowledge, as John 20:9 does, the importance of the written Word as an authoritative witness. The narrator's commentary on the formation of the disciples' belief makes clear that the testimony of Scripture (in this case, the Old Testament) is itself essential and irreplaceable evidence for the resurrection of Jesus. Not only does verse 9 explain that Jesus rose from the dead, but it also says he "must" have done so, that this was all part of God's purposeful plan. In this case Scripture adds not only to the "what" but also to the "why." While there is a place for apologetics that relies on historical and philosophical proofs, Christians must be careful not to avoid or minimize the primacy of Scripture for securing belief and its certainties.

THE GARDENER IN THE GARDEN. The narrator clearly wants the reader to see the resurrection of Jesus in this "garden" in light of the original garden in Genesis. Since it was in a garden that the world betrayed God, a garden is a fitting place for his final betrayal and for its overturning. And, just as Mary was wrong to think that Jesus was the gardener, she was also perfectly correct. This was the gardener in his biblical garden, the second Adam. If the first Adam in the garden brought death out of life, the second Adam in the garden brought life out of death. Finally, in this garden the gardener himself came to tend his (new) creation (Gen. 2:15; Revelation 21–22).

Theological Soundings

CHILDREN OF THE FATHER. This miracle account is the first time that the fatherhood of God is applied to the disciples and that familial language is used between the disciples (John 20:17). The Gospel of John began with the promise that God the Son would unite the children of God to God the Father (1:12). Not until the resurrection of Jesus were this access and right fully manifested. This remarkable status reached its fullest provision when the first human of the new creation, the resurrected Jesus, walked out of the tomb. It is for this reason that God's children gather weekly on the "first day of the week" (20:1) and celebrate together Jesus' resurrection, our rest in him, and our fellowship as the family of God.

THE ASCENSION. The Heidelberg Catechism (Q&A 49) suggests three applications we can derive from the ascension of Jesus. First, we have the comfort that the resurrected Lord is also our advocate, interceding on our behalf in heaven before God. Second, the truth that we have our own flesh in heaven is a sure pledge that Christ will take us, his members, up to himself. Third, he will send his Spirit to us on earth as a pledge, a promise, and a guarantee of our inheritance. This explains what can be taken initially as harsh or unsympathetic words of Jesus to Mary in verse 17. Jesus is not limiting Mary's access to him but wants to give her a share in his life by means of the new creation reality that required not only his resurrection but also his ascension. The presence of Christ is now experienced in a new creation manner: in Christ and through the Spirit. Such a relation to Jesus is more intimate than anything experienced prior to his ascension.

Personal Implications

Take some time to reflect on what you have learned from your study of John 20:1–18 and how it might apply to your own life today. Make notes below on the personal implications for your walk with the Lord of the (1) *Gospel Glimpses*, (2) *Whole-Bible Connections*, (3) *Theological Soundings*, and (4) this passage as a whole.

1. Gospel Glimpses

2. Whole-Bible Connections

3. Theological Soundings

4. John 20:1–18

As You Finish This Unit . . .

As the church declares regularly, "Jesus is risen! His is risen indeed!" Take a moment to look back through this study and reflect on the many things the Lord may be teaching you.

Definitions

[1] **Sabbath** – Originally Saturday, the seventh day of the week, the Jewish day of worship and rest (Gen. 2:2–3; Ex. 31:13–17). Now Christians meet for worship on Sunday, the day of Christ's resurrection (Acts 20:7), and regard Sunday, rather than Saturday, as their weekly day of rest as they look forward to an eternal Sabbath rest (Heb. 4:1–13).

[2] **Ascension** – The departure of the resurrected Jesus to God the Father in heaven (Luke 24:50–51; Acts 1:1–12).

Week 12: Summary and Conclusion

In this final study we will consider the miracles of Jesus as a whole and the important role they play in the way Christians think and live. There will also be an opportunity to review some of your most important reflections from the various *Gospel Glimpses*, *Whole-Bible Connections*, and *Theological Soundings* encountered through this study.

The Big Picture of the Miracles of Jesus

We began this study by challenging the common assumption that a miracle is something that occurs contrary to nature. While a miracle may be contrary to what is known of nature, as Augustine suggested it is certainly something that belongs to the realm of nature. The reason is made clear in Scripture: the natural world is God's creation, which he orders according to his providence and purposes. We are not wrong, however, to define miracles as "extraordinary operations" of God that intervene in what we perceive to be the natural operations of creation. For that reason miracles are more communicative to us in their power and even purpose. Miracles direct us to look at or think about something in a specific way and for a special reason: the person and work of Jesus Christ.

Rooted in the foundational miracle of the exodus (Exodus 1–18), the first of many "signs" in the unfolding biblical story, the miracles of Jesus do two things: communicate the truth about Jesus and challenge people to trust in him. Miracles not only direct people to the person of Jesus but also summon every person to a decision of faith. Jesus does this by performing hundreds of miracles (over forty are recorded in the Gospels), which span the created order, from old creation to the new. In this way Jesus not only displays his role as Savior and Lord over creation but also enacts the entire biblical story of creation until he inaugurates the renewed creation by means of his own resurrection.

The miracles of Jesus can be seen for their ministerial purpose when they are viewed in relation to the biblical story's order of creation. Many of Jesus' miracles are performed in ways that reflect his sovereign reign over the world as it is now, or what we have called the old creation. Miracles of the old creation include miracles of fertility, healing, destruction, and, in some cases, dominion. Each of those kinds of miracles explains various truths about Jesus' person and work. Miracles of fertility, for example, magnify the ways in which God is the provider for his creation. Miracles of healing, then, declare God to be the sustainer of his creation. In what might seem contradictory but is significant in relation to the holiness of God, miracles of destruction reflect God's supreme right to judge his creation, reflective of his role as Lord and King. Finally, miracles of dominion, as in the stilling of the storm (Mark 4:35–41), reflect God's ongoing and constant power over his creation. These types of miracles, then, present in full color the ways in which God rules over and ministers within his creation and on behalf of his creatures, specifically man.

Other miracles of Jesus reflect his intention to bring forth the world that is to come, or what we have called the new creation. Miracles of the new creation include some miracles of dominion but primarily involve miracles of reversal and glorification. Like the miracles of the old creation, each of those kinds of miracles explains truths about Jesus' person and work. But in this case it is a ministry that presents and provides a true redemption of the sinful realities of the old creation. For example, one aspect of the miracles of dominion, such as walking on water (Matt 14:22–33), reflects God's intentions to renew and perfect his people into a new human nature. Miracles of reversal express Jesus' dominion more strongly and reflect his authority and intention to renew all of creation. Finally, miracles of glorification, specifically the resurrection of Jesus, announce the beginning of the new creation in the actual body of our resurrected Lord. These types of miracles, like their counterparts, present the ways in which God is ministering in the world in such a way so as to bring forth a new, perfect world, which he promised from the beginning.

When we study the miracles of Jesus, therefore, we are following the whole biblical story and its ultimate goal of the renewal of all creation. The miracles of Jesus show how the work of the Creator at the beginning of the world is ongoing and magnified especially in the life and ministry of Jesus as he redeems his creation from its brokenness and establishes the promised and perfect world to come. The miracles of Jesus also yield a very practical perspective for the disciples of Jesus. Since the miracles of Jesus fall within the context of creation, we are taught to see every aspect of creation through the lens of the loving and redeeming work of our Lord Jesus Christ. Jesus' miracles not only explain him but challenge us to trust him. We are pastored to trust, wait, hope, and even lament in light of Christ's purposes and promises as we wait for the redemption of the world and the glory of the new creation.

Read through the following three sections on *Gospel Glimpses*, *Whole-Bible Connections*, and *Theological Soundings*. Then take time to consider the *Personal Implications* these sections have for you.

Gospel Glimpses

It is not uncommon for Christians to think the miracles of Jesus are intended to serve as apologetic proofs of Jesus' divinity. As much as Jesus truly is God, the miracles communicate more than his divine identity and ability. The miracles explain the ministry of Jesus and therefore the gospel. The miracles show how Jesus engages and confronts a fallen, broken creation and its creatures and brings healing and redemption in a way that reflects the message of good news revealed progressively in Scripture. In this way the miracles teach us about the ministry of Jesus to redeem and heal his creation, specifically his people.

Review the *Gospel Glimpses* in each section of this study. Each of Jesus' miracles directs our attention to the grace of God provided through Jesus, often in the very details of the miracle story. What are two or three lessons you learned about the kind of grace Jesus provides to us?

As you reflect on the many ways Jesus provides his people with the grace of God through his miraculous works, what is one profound truth about God's grace you learned from this study that motivates you to praise him?

Whole-Bible Connections

The miracles of Jesus offer a retelling of the entire story of the Bible, the complete account of the ways in which God ministers to his creation. This is why it is helpful to classify the miracles according to old creation or new creation, primarily since the miracles reflect God's intention to care for his creation and bring forth the new creation through the redemptive and completive work of Jesus Christ. The miracles of Jesus, then, provide us with lenses to see the full story of Scripture and the ways the parts connect to the whole. Every individual miracle is, in reality, a subset of the ultimate miracle of the originating and perfecting of creation.

As you review the *Whole-Bible Connections* throughout the study, identify two or three themes that you find especially helpful for your big-picture understanding of the Bible.

The exodus is the foundational "miracle" in the Bible, the first biblical sign upon which all the miracles of Jesus are built. Moses reflects Jesus as he reveals God and proclaims the ministry of redemption God will accomplish. Read the accounts in the exodus story of when the miracles are first depicted as "signs" in Exodus 4:1–9 and 7:1–7. What do the exodus miracles proclaim about God, and how is the use of *sign* in Exodus similar to its use in relation to the miracles of Jesus in the Gospels (see John 20:30–31)?

Theological Soundings

While all Scripture is needed to explain that which God has revealed about his character and purposes, the miracles of Jesus offer a unique perspective on the core doctrines of the Christian faith, notably the doctrine of God. The miracles display the compassion and intentionality of Jesus as he engages in our broken world and redeems it with his grace and power. The miracles are a perfect blend of grace and truth, with the latter reflecting the theological truths that the miracles teach us about God.

Review the *Theological Soundings* throughout this study. List several doctrinal insights that were new to you or that challenged your understanding of God.

Reflect on how the miracles of Jesus taught you about the person and character of God. In what ways did Jesus show both grace and truth as he dealt with the brokenness of creation and brought healing and redemption? How does Jesus minister in similar ways now in our broken world and lives?

Reflect on how the miracles teach us about both Jesus' divinity and his humanity. In what ways do the miracles of Jesus explain and confirm that Jesus is God? How do the miracles also explain and reflect his humanity, and in what ways does this expand your view of Jesus?

Personal Implications

The miracles magnify for us the brokenness of our creation and its creatures, as well as the authority and mercy of our Lord Jesus Christ. As we conclude this study, write down some final lines of application for yourself individually and for the church collectively.

What do the miracles of Jesus reveal about the consequences of sin in our world and even in the bodies of its creatures? In what ways does the reality of sin's consequences help you fight against sin in your own life as it also pushes you toward Jesus?

How do the miracles of Jesus aid your ability to trust in Christ with your own battle with the consequences of sin? How has this study changed how you look at or deal with sickness and even death?

How do the miracles of Jesus, especially his resurrection, give you renewed hope in the certainty and glory of the coming new creation? Does the reality of complete healing and redemption in the new creation help you live differently or with a better perspective now?

As You Finish Studying the Miracles of Jesus . . .

We rejoice with you as you finish studying the miracles of Jesus! May this study become part of your Christian walk of faith, day by day and week by week throughout all your life. Now we would greatly encourage you to study the

Word of God on a week-by-week basis. To continue your study of the Bible we encourage you to consider other books in the *Knowing the Bible* series and to visit www.crossway.org/knowingthebible.

Be encouraged to review this study from time to time. Revisit the notes you have written and the things you have highlighted or underlined. Reflect again on the key themes that the Lord has been teaching you about himself and his Word. May these things become a treasure for you throughout your life—which we pray will be true for you, in the name of the Father and the Son and the Holy Spirit. Amen.

KNOWING THE BIBLE STUDY GUIDE SERIES

Experience the *Grace* of God in the *Word* of God

Series Volumes

- Genesis
- Exodus
- Leviticus
- Numbers
- Deuteronomy
- Joshua
- Judges
- Ruth and Esther
- 1–2 Samuel
- 1–2 Kings
- 1–2 Chronicles
- Ezra and Nehemiah
- Job
- Psalms
- Proverbs
- Ecclesiastes
- Song of Solomon
- Isaiah
- Jeremiah
- Lamentations, Habakkuk, and Zephaniah
- Ezekiel
- Daniel
- Hosea
- Joel, Amos, and Obadiah
- Jonah, Micah, and Nahum
- Haggai, Zechariah, and Malachi
- Matthew
- Mark
- Luke
- John
- Acts
- Romans
- 1 Corinthians
- 2 Corinthians
- Galatians
- Ephesians
- Philippians
- Colossians and Philemon
- 1–2 Thessalonians
- 1–2 Timothy and Titus
- Hebrews
- James
- 1–2 Peter and Jude
- 1–3 John
- Revelation
- The Parables of Jesus
- The Sermon on the Mount
- The Ten Commandments
- Jesus' Farewell Discourse
- Jesus' Speech on the Mount of Olives
- The Miracles of Jesus

crossway.org/knowingthebible